PRAISE FOR *STICKABILITY*

"This book reminds us that with a Positive Mental Attitude,
all things are possible."

—JIM OLESON, president of The Napoleon Hill Foundation

"A fantastic read."

—LOU FERRIGNO, bodybuilder and actor on *The Incredible Hulk*, TV series

"Another great release from
The Napoleon Hill Foundation—outstanding!"

—MIKE HELTON, president of NASCAR

"To succeed in life and business, we all need *Stickability*."

—BRIAN TRACY, international bestselling author

"This book is worth its weight in gold."

—RICHARD COHN, Beyond Words Publishing, publisher of *The Secret*

"To achieve the success you truly deserve, read this book today."

—JAMES AMOS, chairman of Tasti D-Lite

"Keep this book on your nightstand and read it daily."

—BOB PROCTOR, founder of LifeSuccess

"Every patriotic, free-enterprising American must read,
absorb, and use this timely wisdom."

—MARK VICTOR HANSEN, cocreator of *Chicken Soup for the Soul*

"*Stickability* is an important reminder
toward the power of perseverance."

—LES BROWN, The Motivator

"*Stickability* is an inspiring read, and I recommend it highly."

—DAVE LINIGER, cofounder of RE/MAX

"The perfect book at the perfect time!"

—TRACEY JONES, president of Tremendous Life Books

"The information contained in this book is both poignant
and illuminating. Read it, use it, and see what
a difference it will make in your life."

—HARRY PAUL, coauthor of *Fish!*

"Mr. [Napoleon] Hill would not only approve of this book,
but would promote it with vigor."

—DAVID M. CORBIN, author of *Illuminate*

"*Stickability* is like food for the soul."

—DAVE BLANCHARD, CEO of Og Mandino Group

Stickability

Stickability

—◦◦◦—

The Power of Perseverance:
The Think and Grow Rich® Series

Greg S. Reid

authorized by

The Napoleon Hill Foundation

JEREMY P. TARCHER/PENGUIN
a member of Penguin Group (USA)
New York

JEREMY P. TARCHER/PENGUIN
Published by the Penguin Group
Penguin Group (USA) LLC
375 Hudson Street
New York, New York 10014

USA • Canada • UK • Ireland • Australia
New Zealand • India • South Africa • China

penguin.com
A Penguin Random House Company

Most Tarcher/Penguin books are available at special quantity discounts for bulk purchase for sales
promotions, premiums, fund-raising, and educational needs. Special books or book excerpts also
can be created to fit specific needs. For details, write: Special.Markets@us.penguingroup.com.

The Library of Congress has catalogued the hardcover edition as follows:

Reid, Greg S.
Think and grow rich : stickability, the power of perseverance / Greg
S. Reid ; authorized by The Napoleon Hill Foundation.
p.   cm.
ISBN 978-0-399-16582-5
1. Success—Case studies.   2. Success in business—Case studies.
3. Perseverance (Ethics)—Case studies.   I. Title.
BF637.S8R386   2013   2013016746
650.1—dc23

ISBN 978-0-399-16886-4 (paperback)

Printed in the United States of America
1   3   5   7   9   10   8   6   4   2

BOOK DESIGN BY TANYA MAIBORODA

Contents

Introduction

—⟨•/•/•⟩—

The Key to All Great Achievements

by J. B. Hill, grandson of Napoleon Hill

WORDS OF WISDOM, AGE-OLD ADAGES, MYTHS AND folktales—whatever we call them, the stories we tell one another and pass down to the next generation connect us across race, religion, and national boundaries. Although these stories have diverse themes, each is powered by the testimony of example, and no story resonates so universally as the tale of how to succeed in life.

But what does this mean? For most of us, it is the application of the experience of others to our own lives. Samuel Smiles, a Scottish author, wrote the first book about success in 1859. Appropriately titled *Self Help*, it laid the framework for the writings of Orison Swett Marden, and later Napoleon Hill, by teaching success through the parables of experience. Napoleon Hill, who is arguably the founder of the modern-day success movement, was a master storyteller who compiled the first comprehensive philosophy of success. He did this after discovering that the most remarkable self-made men of his time— like Andrew Carnegie, Thomas Edison, and Henry Ford—all did the same thing to succeed, although they each used different means.

For the past 150 years, success philosophers and thinkers have proved time and again that one trait in particular appears to be a key to all great achievement—*persistence*. It was persistence that allowed George Goethals to build the Panama Canal when so many had failed. It was persistence that drove Edison to success in devising a viable lightbulb. It was persistence that pushed Abraham Lincoln through a broken heart, two business failures, and eight losses for election to public office to become president of the United States. Napoleon Hill wrote:

> One reason why most men seldom accumulate fortunes until they have passed well beyond the 40-year goal post of life is that *they must undergo* failures and adversities and overcome sufficient obstacles to develop in them sufficient knowledge to accumulate wealth.

Therefore, it is those who persist and learn from failure who carve their place in history.

As I read *Stickability*, I was reminded of a boy I knew more than fifty years ago named Scott Shaw. He was my playmate during early adolescence and was perhaps the most obnoxious kid in the world. One day, our jostling turned into a knockdown fight. There was no one around to cheer us on or to stop the fight. So we fought as boys do, until we didn't fight anymore. I was bigger and stronger than he was and I kept knocking him down. But every time Scott went down, he got up and came at me.

With bloody lip, tears flowing from his eyes, and snot dripping from his nose, he kept getting off the ground and coming at me. He took everything I dished out, and still he came at me, time after time. After he got off the ground for the last time, he was met with my hand, offering him a handshake. Mastered, I said, "You win, Scott . . . you win." He glared at me, wiped his nose, stifled a tear, and shook my hand. We were friends until I moved away a few years later.

Stickability is full of stories about people like Scott Shaw— men and women who refused to submit to defeat. It is a delightful book, written with the same energy, impact, and simplicity as *Outwitting the Devil* and *Think and Grow Rich: Three Feet from Gold*. This new Napoleon Hill Foundation book shares insight from the people who have helped shape our world. They are the leaders who began a pathway to success with nothing more than an idea to follow. Their goals may not be your goals, and their setbacks and failures are not yours either. However, their stories are parables of success that will inspire you to find *your* own road to personal achievement.

Stickability reinforces the proven success principles that were compiled by my grandfather, Napoleon Hill, during his lifetime by providing valuable, thought-provoking insight from the lives of incredible people. Their stories demonstrate that a definite goal strengthened by persistence will always lead to success. They show that "negatives" are just the tasks that need to be done to avoid a setback and that setbacks should be viewed as *opportunities* to reroute a path to success.

This is the book to pick off a shelf and read and reread during those discouraging moments when the temptation to quit looms larger than the desire for success. It is a book that clearly explains why Napoleon Hill wrote, "Most great people have attained their greatest success just one step BEYOND their greatest setback and failure."

So when the time comes to refocus, redirect, and recommit (as it surely will), take a copy off the shelf, put your feet up for an hour or so, and read *Stickability* again. It is a small price for success.

Stickability

CHAPTER 1

The Three Causes
of Failure

YOU'VE SEEN THOSE INFOMERCIALS. THE ONES THAT
make elaborate claims like:

> "You too can make money in real estate and be a mogul
> like me! Buy our 30-day course and we'll make you an
> instant millionaire."

Maybe you've even bought a book that promised to change
your life overnight, or attended a seminar to learn the latest
investment tips to become financially independent *in no time*.

Both late-night TV and local bookstores are filled with the
latest and greatest "get rich" opportunities that are guaranteed
to succeed. Each novel idea is larger than the next. Whether it's

stocks, bonds, real estate, or what have you, the solution is always the same: Follow these simple, easy steps and watch your bank account grow with little effort.

Thus, happiness is achieved.

The leaps from get-rich-quick to success to happiness are there, although they are implied, for the most part. They are nestled in between the lines of stories that have little relevance to *your* power—which is the power to define what it is you want.

Get-rich-quick narratives distract us from this. We are then left only to adopt someone else's goal and perhaps quit halfway to achieving it. Obstacles are only as insurmountable as your goal—your *want*—is weak.

Unfortunately, these narratives rarely tell us that success is seldom easy. The fact is that we will have to face challenges and obstacles in order to achieve most goals. They forget to mention that unexpected circumstances are inevitable, and more important that how we accept, deny, or capitalize on these circumstances is entirely up to us—and will ultimately determine our success or failure.

Every individual who has attained personal achievement can tell you that the question is not *will* there be tough times, the question is *when* will they arrive? It's through these moments of uncertainty that our character is revealed.

For many, the first sign of difficulties can be enough for them to become discouraged and stop doing what they intended, while others find the determination to discover another way to prevail. Rather than giving up, they look for the opportunity *within* the challenge—and it's there, always. Some opportunities are buried deep within the challenge. Others are easy to find. The extent to which we're able to slow down, breathe, and adopt perspective is the extent to which we're able to find the opportunity within the challenge. We're then in a much better position to overcome any challenge and achieve whatever it is we want to achieve.

Make no mistake—adopting perspective in the face of challenge is not easy. This in itself is the challenge.

We can agree that we all want happiness and prosperity in our lives, and also know that . . .

Happiness takes discipline.

To achieve happiness we must first have the discipline to determine carefully what this means for us. Once we have a clearly defined goal, we must maintain discipline to find the opportunities within the challenges we'll face along the way. This is when we make strides in what we call *self-development*.

Think about it. It's easy to be happy-go-lucky and make great decisions when everything is going our way. The question is, how do we respond when a challenge comes? It's at this precise moment that who we are as people is revealed to the world, and to us. When we quit, we automatically *fail*—meaning simply that we do not achieve a goal. Yet, when we accept the challenge, we're able to clearly understand the reason(s) for the challenge, find the opportunity, and continue on a different path.

How we handle temporary setbacks will ultimately determine our outcome.

Remember this: whether it's a weed in the garden, a dream, desire—or even fear—what we feed and focus attention on will eventually grow the most. The same applies to opportunity. What we focus on is what we see. When one seeks the good, good things happen. When one seeks opportunity, opportunities occur.

When it comes to financial matters, for example, you may fixate on media buzz or a temporary dip in the market, get anxious, and veer from your long-term intention by selling your interest. Alternatively, someone else may see a golden opportunity to take advantage of the dip and buy more at a lower rate.

The realities are the same for us all. Yes, the market may be the lowest in years, yet where one person sees only loss and challenge, another sees opportunity and possibility.

Just the fact that you are reading this shows you are smart enough to know that somewhere along life's journey, a wrench will be thrown into the gears. It also shows that you are intelligent enough to know right from wrong.

When hurdles arise, will you cut corners or stay the course? Will you fudge the numbers or keep what's true? You can see someone's true self simply by observing how they act when they're faced with a difficult situation and think no one is watching.

And someone is *always* watching, even when we're not aware of it.

Moral philosopher and political economist Adam Smith introduced the concept of the *impartial spectator* to help us understand this phenomenon. The impartial spectator refers to the general notion that we all have of what is commonly expected of us. In this sense, society's expectations act as a body of surveillance that affects our actions and thoughts. When we are faced with challenges, our reactions expose our true character to others specifically, and to the impartial spectator generally. This is why it is crucial to know clearly who we are and who we want to be. Seizing opportunities within challenges exposes a character of strength, resolve, patience and, yes, *stickability*.

Let's look at *success* from a different perspective and turn the principle upside down. Rather than focus on and illustrate another surefire blueprint for abundance, as mentioned earlier, let's place our attention on its counterpart: *failure*, and its often forgotten component, *missed opportunity*.

It's been suggested that personal achievement eventually comes from focusing on our *major definite purpose* (some call it passion) and then from the courage and *stickability* to see that vision through.

Those of us who are familiar with this concept from Napoleon Hill may be surprised to find that he also had brilliant insights into *failure* and *challenges* that have gone relatively unnoticed in subsequent decades.

Let's take a look back . . .

In 1938, one year after releasing what many refer to as the bible of personal development, *Think and Grow Rich*, Dr. Hill was interviewed on a syndicated radio program. He examined the topic of failure from a unique perspective that has gone unpublished until today.

The following excerpts reveal in his own words what he referred to as the Three Causes of Failure.

In an unwavering discussion, Hill explained how three habits can either ruin a person's dreams or be redirected and transformed into stepping-stones for success.

When asked what the causes of failure are, Hill answered:

"Cause of failure number one is *the inability to get along with other people.*

"Regardless of how well educated you may be, or how responsible your job may be, or how much money you may have, if you can't induce people to like you, if you can't get along with all sorts of people under all sorts of circumstances, you can never become a great success in any undertaking."

Hill was asked, "What can you do to make people like you?"

He explained, "The first step you must take in causing people to like you is by liking them, and expressing it in the tone of your voice, in a pleasant smile when you are speaking to others, and in a sincere desire to be helpful to others whether they deserve it or not."

This first cause of failure may seem simple to avoid, yet it is an art to really learn to love people and become loveable. The more you work on developing your personality, the easier you'll interact with those around you.

Think about it this way: the best way to get others interested in you is to show interest in them. Consider this. If folks take an interest in a story you tell at a party, you are far more likely to show interest in their stories, right? The same applies to others as applies to you.

You are not alone.

According to what's known as the Gaia Principle, the earth is a living, breathing organism. The theory posits that each and every component of this organism—including humans—is connected to every other component for survival. In spite of the relatively recent explosion of *individualism*, we must reestablish the fundamental value of working with others. It is a skill, to be sure. You were not born with or without the necessary skills to get along with others. These skills are learned. We must continuously hone what's known today as *people skills* to succeed in any area of life.

"It is impossible to be successful on your own," Hill declared. "The better you get along with others and are able to induce them to work with you, the more you'll be able to achieve. You can't be quick to judge, overly critical, or look down on people."

Continuing, Hill explained:

"The second cause of failure is a very common one, the habit of *quitting* when the going is hard. No matter who you are or how skilled you may be in your occupation, there will be times when the going is hard, and unpleasant circumstances will overtake you. Now, if you yield easily to these obstacles you may as well write yourself off as far as becoming a great success is concerned. When you meet with opposition of any nature, instead of quitting, you should turn on more willpower;

kill the fires with stronger faith in your own ability while making up your mind that you will not sell yourself short, and eventually you will succeed."

It bears repeating: do not sell yourself short!

You deserve everything you seek. *Know* this, and you are well on your way. But being *on the way* to success is clearly not enough. How many times have we quit too soon? Often there is just one more step needed, but we fail to see this because we are too preoccupied with the challenge itself—and not the solution.

Napoleon Hill said that if he could choose one trait to instill in each person it would be the *persistence* to keep going when the going gets hard. These are the moments when the greatest achievements have been realized.

In a personal meeting, Thomas Edison told Napoleon Hill how he reacted to failure when striving to perfect the incandescent electric lamp. As history tells it, it took Edison hundreds of failed attempts before he triumphed. The average person would likely have quit after a few attempts. Could it be, as Napoleon Hill suggested, that this is why there is only one Thomas Edison and so many average people?

During the radio interview, Napoleon Hill went on to say, "All successful people in the higher brackets make it their habit to *create* circumstances and opportunities favorable to themselves instead of accepting whatever life offers them."

Life is not something that just happens to you. You are not merely a reactor. You are an actor. Of course, you can't always control your circumstances, but you can control how you deal with them.

When the host asked what happens to those who quit, who fail to turn these circumstances into opportunities, Hill replied, "The act of *procrastination* is the third cause of failure.

"You need to be able to discern when a great opportunity presents itself and act immediately. You could miss out on one of the best things that could ever happen to you because you don't see the potential of what you are being offered, or because you procrastinate in making the right decision."

It's possible that this single act could change your life forever. Humans are decision makers. The process of making decisions—what we call *reason* or *rationality*—is what gives us our unique power. Always keep in mind that the worst decision often is making no decision at all.

Indecision and procrastination can exact a high price, as is proven by the story of an automobile manufacturing company that decided to begin an extensive expansion program. (We assume this was Ford Motor Company, though Hill never specified.)

As Hill tells it:

"The president of the largest automotive manufacturing

plant called in one hundred young men from the various departments of the facility and said to them, 'Gentlemen, we are going to enlarge our plant and greatly increase our output of automobiles, which means that we will need executives and department managers far beyond our present staff. We are offering each of you the privilege of working four hours per day in the office, where you will learn to become executives, and four hours at your regular jobs in the plant. There will be some homework, and there may be times when you will have to forgo your social duties and work overtime. Your pay will be the same that you are now getting in the plant. I am passing out cards on which I wish each of you who will accept our offer to write your name. I will give you one hour in which to talk among yourselves and make up your minds.'"

Surely, all of the one hundred men would accept such an incredible opportunity, a chance of a lifetime—wouldn't they? No, they didn't. At that time, only twenty-three out of the hundred men accepted the opportunity given by the president of the company. The following day, thirty more men came forward and said they wanted to accept the offer.

Napoleon Hill continued the story: "The president said, 'Gentlemen, you were given one hour in which to make up your minds after you had all of the facts concerning my offer. I am very sorry but this opportunity is gone forever. I have learned from experience that the man who cannot or will not make up his mind quickly and definitely when he has all of the necessary facts to enable him to do so, will change his mind quickly at the first sign of obstacles, or he will allow other people to talk him into changing his mind.' This was the case for those who changed their minds. They consulted their wives or others to help them decide."

Hill had experienced firsthand the importance of being decisive thirty years earlier, when he first met Andrew Carnegie.

"I went to see Mr. Carnegie to write a success story for a magazine based on his stupendous achievements. Originally, he allotted me three hours for the interview, but actually it lasted three days and nights during which he was interviewing me with a purpose in mind without my knowing what he was up to. During those three days, he was telling me that the world needed a new success philosophy, one that would give the average man or woman the full benefit of all that he and other successful men like himself had learned from a lifetime of experience.

"Mr. Carnegie said it was a sin of major proportions that successful men allowed their hard-earned experience to be buried with their bones. Then at the end of the third day, Mr. Carnegie said, 'Now, I have been talking to you for three days about the need for a simple success philosophy. I am going to ask you one question which I want you to answer with a simple yes or no, but don't answer it until you make up your mind definitely. If I commission you to organize the world's first particular success philosophy, will you devote twenty years to research and interview successful people, and earn your own way so you go along without a financial subsidy from me? Yes or no?'

"I said, 'Yes, Mr. Carnegie, I'll accept your offer and you may depend upon it, sir, that I will carry it out to the finish.' Mr. Carnegie said, 'All right, you have the job, and I like the mental attitude in which you accepted the assignment.'"

Later, Hill learned that Carnegie was timing his future protégé with a stopwatch held behind his desk, allowing sixty seconds for him to make up his mind. Napoleon Hill used twenty-nine of those seconds to give his answer.

In just twenty-nine seconds, Hill changed his life and created the first-ever formula for success.

Hill went on to explain: "Andrew Carnegie believed that a person not capable of making prompt decisions is a person unable to carry out important assignments. But, that wasn't all. There was another quality that Mr. Carnegie was in search of, the habit of turning on more willpower instead of quitting when the going is hard. Mr. Carnegie knew that there is always a time in every undertaking when one meets with obstacles and is overtaken by opposition, and he recognized that the quitter never wins and the winner never quits."

At this historic meeting, Napoleon Hill made the decision to do twenty years of research to identify the success philosophy for which he is now famous.

During the radio show, the host asked his guest whether he had faced obstacles along the way.

Napoleon Hill responded:

"My greatest obstacle was friends and relatives who believed I had undertaken too big a job. They chided me for working for the richest man in the world for twenty years without financial compensation from him, and one of the queer traits of most people, especially one's own relatives, is that they so often discourage any member of the family who steps out ahead of the crowd and aspires to achieve outstanding success. I learned that when one needs anything very badly, it is very difficult for him to find anyone who wishes to help him get it, but when one gets over the hump, achieves recognition, and no longer needs help, well then about everybody on earth wants to do something for him.

"*Every failure, every adversity, and every unpleasant circumstance carries with it the seed of equivalent benefit or advantage.*

"The person who has a sound philosophy to live by learns

very quickly how to find this seed of equivalent benefit and to germinate it into advantage. And as far as *luck* is concerned, it may be true that it often plays a temporary role in the lives of people. But remember this truth: if luck may offer temporary defeat or failure, one doesn't have to accept this as a permanent result. By searching for that seed of equivalent benefit one may actually transform a failure into an enduring success."

Napoleon Hill's advice is that we apply the lessons he shared to best fit our own lives.

How many great opportunities may you have missed because you didn't get along with the person who could help you achieve your goals, you gave up too soon, or you took too long to decide, or even allowed another to talk you out of your desire?

Now that you know about Napoleon Hill's Three Causes of Failure, you can avoid making these mistakes in your own quest for achievement.

HOW? LET'S LOOK AT THEM, ONE BY ONE.

The Inability to Get Along with Other People

GENUINELY take interest in other people's success. Do not act on immediate feelings of competition or jealousy. Just because someone else achieves what you consider to be success doesn't mean that you cannot succeed as well. Success is not finite. Despite the analogy of "taking a slice of the American pie," another person's success does not in any way compromise your success potential. Be proud of other people's success, especially those closest to you. When we improve our communication skills and sincerely care for other people, these same individuals will become more willing to help us along as well.

Quitting

ALWAYS REMEMBER: "Quitters never win, and winners never quit." It's likely you've heard this from others before reading this book, and there is a reason this philosophy is so pervasive. Words matter, and this is as simple and true as it gets. When you feel like giving up, focus on the outcome rather than the struggle—and push yourself to keep going, no matter how difficult this may seem. Be careful to evaluate your goal. If it's the right goal for you, you are unlikely to act on the urge to quit in the face of challenges. You will reap the rewards when you have the courage and *stickability* to see your vision through.

Procrastination

GET IN TOUCH with your definite purpose so you may discern quickly when a great opportunity presents itself. Be decisive and take immediate action! Remember that sometimes the worst decision is making no decision at all. Don't allow self-doubt to stop you. The greatest achievers are those who seize opportunities when they present themselves. These are the individuals who do not have self-doubt, but self-confidence. Have the confidence that is needed to take on a job or an assignment that may seem overwhelming at first. Put another way: have faith in yourself!

CHAPTER 2

Flexibility Is Key

FEW PRODUCTS HAVE SHAPED OUR LIVES AS MUCH AS the cell phone. The pace at which we can access information, accomplish tasks, and interact with one another has dramatically increased since the introduction of this mobile device and its even more sophisticated cousin, the smartphone.

Can you imagine what your life would be like without your cell phone? It has given us some of life's ultimate gifts—freedom, time, and knowledge, as well as mobility. Do you realize that this single creation has given those of us alive today more opportunity than any generation that has gone before us?

It's become the great equalizer.

With the evolution of smartphones, even people who live

below the poverty line in the United States have greater access to knowledge at their fingertips than fills the Library of Congress. According to an International Telecommunication Union report in 2011, 6 billion people worldwide (87 percent of the world population) have cell-phone subscriptions, and more than 60 percent of all cell-phone users are in developing nations. It's been estimated that a fourteen-year-old kid with a smartphone now has access to more information in his pocket than the president of the United States did a mere eighteen years ago.

Right now, all the information needed to accomplish anything we could ever imagine lies within our palm—literally— thanks to the brilliant mind of a man who saw an opportunity before anyone else: Martin Cooper.

Credited as the inventor of the modern-day cellular phone, Martin Cooper is a visionary, and an excellent example of *stickability*. He took advantage when the opportunity presented itself. He didn't procrastinate, but took continued action against doubters and unparalleled obstacles.

Martin understood that great ideas originate from one of three things:

- A need
- An unsolved problem
- An easier way of doing things

Solutions are created by a person or team with the ability to address one of these points, and with the persistence to see that vision through. This point is needed most when inventing new ideas, as there is no road map to follow. (Wait till you get to the chapter about Steve Wozniak and his role in the creation of Apple computers!)

Martin Cooper began by developing portable products, including the first handheld police radios, made for the Chicago police department, and citywide pagers, which led to the invention of the first 800 MHz cellular phone, often called the "Brick," in 1973.

You remember those big devices on *Miami Vice* that weighed about 2.5 pounds each? Sure, there were car phones at the time, but nobody thought that having a portable phone would be of any value. Martin, however, saw things differently and envisioned a phone that would be so portable it could go anywhere.

After countless hours of trial and error, and in defiance of skeptics, Martin eventually became the first person in history to make a public call using what he referred to as a "personal telephone."

Standing in the streets of New York City, he picked up the phone to dial. And yet, who could he call? No one else had a portable device!

After a moment of contemplation he decided to call the

only logical person at a landline number: his chief competitor at Bell Labs. Motorola (the company Martin worked for) had just beaten Bell Labs to make the first apparatus work, and Martin wasn't shy about letting them know it.

Just like the "shot heard 'round the world," this insurgence caused a huge market shift toward the *person* and away from the *place*. Martin saw the demand for people to be able to communicate wherever they are, without the need for the traditional copper wire.

In 2006, Martin Cooper and his wife, Arlene Harris (an ingenious innovator in her own right), founded GreatCall, makers of the Jitterbug cell phone, in cooperation with the Verizon network. Here, Arlene tapped her own extensive background from her previous employment, and the two built a company that provided mobile telephone service on its own proprietary brand of handsets. They marketed it to the elderly and to others looking for simplicity—a true modern example of applying the "Keep It Simple, Stupid" (KISS) formula in a practical and successful manner.

What was the secret behind their success? He understood that:

Stickability *has to be consistent with flexibility.*

A balance is crucial. Martin said that sometimes you can take *stickability* too far. It's important to know the difference between perseverance and stubbornness.

You have to be able to adjust if necessary. This means, of course, that you first have to be able to identify when adjustments need to be made. You must be fair and open with yourself. Sometimes this includes listening to others' feedback, even when you don't wish to hear it.

According to Martin, obstacles can do one of two things.

One: they can make you quit.

Two: they can reinforce your resolution.

Again, it's the undeniable difference that sets apart those who succeed and those who fail. For many, the obstacle is the failure—and they stop. But for those who see the achievement, the obstacle is simply a means to a better solution. It is as simple as having perspective:

In the past, the future depended on changes around us.
Today, the future depends on the changes within us.

Martin continues: "Once we latch onto something that has potential, we must always adapt, always keep moving, and the easiest way to do so is by not fearing failure. And of course . . .

become a great student of success. For myself, when I got frustrated I simply shadowed those I admired most, looked for strengths I could incorporate myself, and then simply applied and emulated those results."

Thank goodness he didn't quit. Can you imagine a life without immediate access to information and to people? A life without texting?

How many creations in our lives would we not have today if the inventors had let obstacles stop them?

What would your life look like if you had quit after the first failed attempt? You would never have learned how to walk, ride a bike, or drive. Do you still have the same level of determination and persistence that you had in your youth to achieve your goals?

When faced with challenges, Martin knew that if one process fell short, another one would eventually succeed. He knew this as a fact; it wasn't something he hoped for. He knew that for every obstacle there was a solution—and he had the *discipline* to find the solution. The solution here is simply never to quit before all options have been exhausted.

And here's the thing: when times are tough and we're obstructed en route to our goals, it may seem that there is no other way to proceed. This is the point at which some quit. While understandable, this is very narrow-minded. In these situations we need perspective. We need to broaden the scope of our thinking and exercise the creativity and discipline to know one thing: there is always another way.

Martin Cooper's thoughts are summarized in this powerful message:

The key is to listen to your inner voice, and outside counsel, while being willing to adjust along the journey.

No story illustrates this better than one about spider monkeys. These creatures are among the quickest and most nimble in the jungle.

As legend has it, a young hunter named San Juan knew his father, grandfather, and many other hunters had tried for decades to catch spider monkeys with spears, nets, and arrows, but the primates were simply too small and agile to conquer. He and his father even made special nets and traps in order to capture their noble foe, but to no avail.

One day San Juan came up with a new idea. He designed a heavy container with a very narrow opening at the top and placed the primate's favorite snack inside. He and the men scattered the containers on the ground and patiently waited to see what would happen.

With eager anticipation, they watched the curious monkeys

climb down from the trees to investigate the containers. The monkeys walked around them, touched them, and then smelled the delicious nuts inside.

What would they do next?

Exactly what San Juan had planned!

The spider monkeys squeezed their little hands through the narrow top of the container to reach inside and grab the treat. Once they wrapped their hands around the nut lying at the bottom of the container, their fists became too large to remove through the tiny opening. Since the containers were too heavy for them to carry off, the monkeys found themselves stuck. San Juan and the men looked on in wonder.

What would the spider monkeys do? Would they let go of the nuts and free themselves, or hold on to the treasure and succumb to capture?

San Juan and the others approached the bewildered monkeys. They witnessed fear in the eyes of the creatures as they came closer, but surprisingly enough the spider monkeys didn't let go of the nuts.

They were unable to adapt to this strange, unforeseen circumstance. They were unable to change course and elude their human predators. The hunters simply snatched them up and locked them in a cage. San Juan was a hero. He had done something nobody had ever done before.

Can you imagine? The spider monkeys were unwilling to let go of a small nut in order to gain their freedom. They had neither the discipline nor the wherewithal to surmount an obstacle that, to us, seems an easy fix: let go of the nut! This is what we mean by *perspective*. What to one may seem like an insurmountable obstacle, to another may seem an easy fix.

Perspective is simpler to achieve when we have unequivocal *faith* that any obstacle can be either overcome or circumvented.

The monkeys could not see a solution beyond their challenge. They simply sat there with their hands stuck in the containers until the hunters captured them. They ended up captive because they didn't have the *flexibility* to adapt to the situation, and they paid for it with their lives.

Could it be that we are no different from the spider monkeys? It's a matter of scale, of course, as most folks would simply let go of the nut in this case. But we're uniquely able to transcend folklore, aren't we?

This is the power of the stories we tell.

Could we be holding on to something that should be let go? Could it be that over time we, too, have confused stubbornness and *stickability*—and ended up just being stuck?

Consider this.

What in your life are you holding on to that might actually be contributing to your demise? It's difficult to immediately determine for certain. Like the nut for the spider monkey, many of the things we hold on to—whether a job, a relationship, a belief system, or what have you—are comfortable, appealing, and seemingly what we desire. This may very well be true, but it takes perspective and self-faith for you to determine without question that the nut in your grasp is worth holding on to.

It may be the case that the very thing you think you want is what's holding you back from accomplishing what you seek.

Ultimately, that's for you to decide.

So breathe.

And consider.

But remember: you're not alone!

———

We sat down with another legendary inventor to shed further light on the importance of being flexible and finding perspective in the face of obstacles.

Ron Klein invented the magnetic strip on the back of your credit/debit card and hotel key, not to mention computerized systems for Multiple Listing Services for realtors, and other great projects that have impacted our lives in many ways.

In an interview, Ron shared, "How you look at problems will make a big difference. It begins with the words we choose. Anything that people may classify as a problem, I choose to refer to as a challenge. A problem is an unbearable blockade, whereas a challenge is an opportunity to find a solution. Plus, you can find a gift behind every challenge."

Complexity is not about the size of the issue, it's about the amount of weight you give it.

"I find solutions by oversimplifying what the challenge is. This is done by asking yourself, what is the *given* (starting point) and what is the *solution* (ending) we are looking for? Look at the conflict and focus on the solution. But don't get caught in the in-between gray area, because every situation can be solved by reducing it to a simple, logical form that is understandable."

Most people get stopped in the process rather than realizing that this is just part of the journey. Setbacks and failures teach us what does *not* work, so we can focus on a new solution that *will*. We've all heard of "trial and error," yet often we do not exercise the patience and discipline necessary to see this process through to the end—but this is what it takes!

By following this simple blueprint, Ron Klein came up with inventions that have shaped the way many of us operate on a daily basis.

When asked how he came up with the idea of the magnetic

strip, he explained that back in the day, every month the credit-card companies gave all retailers a list of poor credit risks, which was comprised of thousands of credit-card account numbers. The enormous list resembled an accordion.

Originally, people were given a hard plastic card with raised numbers on it. When a customer came to pay for a purchase, the salesperson had to *manually* go through the entire list to see if the customer's number appeared on the risk alert. The process was very time consuming, especially during the holidays.

Ron felt that the problem could be solved by following his simple process. The *given* was that there were risky accounts, and the *goal* was to mitigate the time needed to check each one.

He recognized that if all of the credit-risk account numbers could be placed in a memory device, then the salesperson could simply key in the account number using a keypad. If the memory device did not flag the customer's account number, the account was fine. This would greatly speed up the process.

But he wasn't satisfied.

To speed it up even more, he felt that "smarts" could be placed into the plastic credit card. He tried this at first by placing coded holes in the card, like those found in a polling card, which would represent the credit-card account number.

Then he discovered a better idea.

Reel-to-reel tape recorders were relatively new at that time, and Ron had a brilliant idea. He theorized that if he pasted a piece of magnetic tape on the back of the card and recorded the account number on the tape, the card could be placed into a small tape reader and the number sent to the memory device to be evaluated. If you inserted the card with the tape attached into the reader and pulled it out rapidly, it would mimic a tape recorder. (This is why you need to slide your card quickly through the reader. It needs to move at the same speed as an old-style reel-to-reel player.)

It worked fine, so Ron went to a company that manufactured plastic credit cards and asked if they could infuse a magnetic material on the back of the cards. They said it was possible. Thus, the Validity Checking System, used for checking the credit status of cardholders, was born.

During our interview, Ron leaned out of his chair and boomed: "You know what the secret is to finding solutions? Look for them!"

What has been his strategy?

"I try to learn something new every day by continually being aware of my environment and paying attention to what people are concerned with. Again, where there is a challenge, there is a solution, and that's what I am looking for. I do this by examining what the given situation is—that is, the starting point—and what solution I'm looking for—in other words, the end destination. *Anything in the middle is superfluous* . . . it's non-important."

In his briefcase Ron carries a worn dictionary. Holding it up, he exclaimed, "See this? What I did was tear out the page that had *problem* and earmarked the page that said *challenge*. Remember, where there is a challenge there is also a solution. The key is to not look over your shoulder and get caught up with the past. Constantly look forward, because you never know how close you could be to a breakthrough—you could be just three feet from gold."

This could be true for many of us.

The real achievement comes from moving forward toward one's dreams and being flexible. This is why it is critical to have the mind-set that you are working toward *progress and not perfection*. As long as you are moving toward success, you are therefore success*ful*. Again, it's progress, not perfection. Just make sure you don't get trapped in the middle.

Imagine driving from Los Angeles to New York City. You know what your starting point is and you know your destination. You get in the car and start driving. Once you have a beginning and an end in mind, what happens in between—road blocks, detours, flat tires, what have you—simply doesn't matter, as long as you stay in motion and keep moving toward your destination. In spite of the challenges you may face, as long as you keep your eye on the *prize* and continue to make progress, eventually you'll end up at your goal.

Proudly, Ron sat back into his seat and said in a calm and easy tone, "Also, enlist others into your dream. Don't be afraid to share your ideas, questions, or fears with others. The same way you would ask for directions when you are lost, or call a mechanic when you have a problem with your car, there are people waiting to assist you along life's journey. All successful people know that they can't succeed by themselves and they need a team. You need to be the leader of your team."

In life and in business, true leaders have one thing in common: they stay cool under fire.

It's the job of the leader to stand strong when others crumble. Their actions are watched so closely that there is little room to flinch when they are faced with challenges over which most people would panic. We look to our leaders to guide and direct us. As a leader you have to stand your ground and stay consistent, because others need to know they can trust and depend on you. Relaxed intensity is thus one of the most important attributes when facing a huge obstacle.

How can you find the right balance?

Understanding the importance of flexibility is the first step.

Know the difference between stickability *and stubbornness.*

LISTEN to feedback with an open mind. Stay focused on your outcome, but be willing to adjust if needed. Don't be a spider monkey holding on to a small nut.

Work toward progress, and don't expect perfection.

ALWAYS keep moving, and keep adapting along the way. When you are afraid to fail, it's impossible to succeed. Create for yourself a safety net for failure. If you allow yourself space to fail you will *learn* from the failure and realize the opportunity within it. Everyone fails—you are not alone. As long as you are moving toward success, consider yourself successful.

Be a great student of success.

YOU DON'T have to reinvent the wheel. By enlisting others into your dream and sharing your ideas, plans, and fears, you can take advantage of experience and feedback from others. Many successful people are happy to share their lessons with you.

CHAPTER 3

Relaxed Intensity
in Action

———

THE ATACAMA DESERT IS ONE OF THE DRIEST AND HARSH-
est regions on earth. People worldwide became familiar with
this barren place on Thursday, August 5, 2010. About 28 miles
north of Copaipó, Chile, a significant accident occurred at the
troubled 121-year-old San José copper and gold mine. You may
remember it.

The buried men, who became known as "Los 33," were
trapped 2,300 feet underground and about three miles from the
mine's entrance via spiraling subterranean service ramps. The
crew of miners and technical support personnel experienced,
among other things, food deprivation and extreme humidity
for an amazing sixty-nine days before their rescue.

"It's been a bit of a long shift," said foreman Luis Urzúa with a smile after his long-awaited rise to the surface. Luis is credited with helping to keep the miners calm and focused on survival during the frightful ordeal.

In his first audio contact with officials on the surface, Luis kept his cool. He didn't mention the hunger and despair he and his men felt, saying, "We're fine, waiting for you to rescue us."

It was perfectly understandable that Luis would be scared. Any of us would be in those conditions—scared to death. But here's the thing: he didn't show it! Instead of panicking, Luis immediately gathered the men in a secure refuge and organized them and their meager resources to cope with the need for long-term survival.

Just after the accident, he led three men to scout the tunnel. After confirming the situation, he made detailed maps of the area to aid the rescue effort. He directed the underground aspects of the rescue operation and coordinated closely with engineers on the surface over teleconference links.

With cool composure he organized a democratic process deep within the earth for all decisions the group needed to make. He empowered the men to take control of an uncontrollable situation.

All thirty-three men survived and credited Luis's composed leadership for maintaining morale and hope. He was able to convert his fear into what we call *relaxed intensity*.

———

From the depths to the heavens . . . a story less well-known is that of Pem Dorjee Sherpa.

At the foot of Mount Everest in Nepal sits a small village called Chyangba. Situated just north of Kathmandu, the isolated township lacks many modern luxuries that most of us take for granted. Development is slow in Chyangba. Comprised of sixty families, the village has no running water and children must walk two hours each way to school every day.

Pem Sherpa grew up in this small corner of the world. Each Friday, people from different ethnic groups—such as Sherpa, Rai, Magar, and Newar—gather to sell their crops or exchange them for rice, tea, salt, oil, butter, or spices. This is a time when villagers come to socialize.

Pem was on his way home one day from visiting his aunt when a beautiful young woman came his way. As she passed by, he smiled at her, and when she smiled back his heart skipped a beat. Thoughts of her consumed Pem. He could hardly sleep that night.

The next day he awoke early. Even in this small village,

Pem was worried he might not find her again. With a racing heart and hopeful mind, he scouted the town, optimistic that he would see her. He searched every corner of the village and at long last his confidence prevailed. When he finally found her, he politely invited her for a walk. He asked where she was from, as he had never before seen her in the village. She told him that she was visiting from Kathmandu.

It didn't take long for the pair to realize there was a connection between them. Even at their young age of barely twenty, they instantly fell in love.

This is normally where the story concludes with "they got married and lived happily ever after." But for Pem, who was Buddhist, and his new love, Shiesma, who was Hindu, things weren't so simple.

In both cultures, it was completely unacceptable to marry outside of your religion and ethnic group. Marriages were not formed out of love. They were arranged by parents who believed they knew what was best for their children. Things such as romance and love came only *after* marriage—once the couple spent some time experiencing life together. Love before marriage was hardly something to consider.

At first, Pem and Shiesma introduced each other to their parents simply as friends. Their elders naturally accepted this and never gave the relationship much thought. They allowed Pem and his friend to visit each other without much fuss. The forbidden lovers met as often as possible. As difficult as it was, hiding their feelings from others fortified their love and made them closer.

One evening Pem visited Shiesma's home for dinner, as he did frequently. When he arrived, however, he immediately sensed something was wrong—something that would change everything.

Shiesma sent an uneasy look at Pem as he entered the house that night. When he asked her what was bothering her, she replied, "Nothing."

"I can tell you are upset, please tell me what is wrong," Pem insisted.

She remained quiet.

"You are not acting like yourself. Please talk to me, you can tell me anything." Pem finally persuaded her to speak up.

She stepped outside, away from her family, to break the news to her trusted friend. Tears flooded her eyes as she looked at the man she loved wholeheartedly.

"My parents have arranged for my marriage."

Pem's heart sank. He could feel the still air surrounding him as the news settled into his now disrupted world. While the news shouldn't have been a surprise to him, he couldn't help but feel the pain. He knew this day would come. Several times before, Shiesma's family had shown Pem pictures of her potential suitors. He had lost his appetite but always maintained composure. He had simply agreed that the suitors looked like nice boys, and continued forcing bites of food into his knotted stomach.

Pem regularly anticipated this day with trepidation. Whenever he'd consider this nightmare, however, he'd shove the fear deep within and move on as if nothing was the matter. But when the day actually arrived, he realized nothing could have prepared him.

What could they do?

Pem comforted Shiesma despite his angst, "Don't worry, I love you. We will find a way to be together."

"How?" Shiesma continued crying. "In only a few weeks I'll be married."

The thought threw another shudder through Pem's body. He knew what he needed to do.

When Shiesma finally calmed down, Pem asked, "Shiesma, I love you. Do you want to marry me?"

A warm smile came over her face. With glowing eyes, she replied, "Yes, Pem! Yes, of course I want to marry you! I love you."

"Okay," Pem continued. "You know this won't be easy. Do you believe our love is strong enough to conquer anything?"

"Yes," Shiesma answered with hope. Pem conveyed to her that he was not going to give up. There was a wedding to plan and nothing was going to stop him.

As the wedding approached, Shiesma became increasingly nervous. She didn't want to have anything to do with the preparations. All she wanted was to marry Pem.

The couple agreed not to see each other for fear of being caught by their families. When Pem finally went to see Shiesma again, they went for a walk as they had done so often. Taking her by the hand, Pem drew his attention upward.

"What do you see over there, Shiesma?" Pem asked as he pointed to the beautiful white snow tops.

"Mount Everest," Shiesma replied.

Pem leaned in close to her, "Mount Everest is viewed as God in both of our religions."

"Yes," Sheisma agreed, waiting for the conclusion.

Pem paused for a moment and took Shiesma's hand in his own. "Do you want to marry me on the top of Mount Everest?"

He expected a delay in her response, as it was an audacious move, but she barely hesitated before exclaiming, "Pem, that is a great idea! Neither of our families will be able to declare our marriage invalid." Pem could see relief in her eyes.

As the day of the arranged marriage drew close, Pem and Shiesma secretly set out on an expedition that would change their lives forever.

Although his new fiancée had no experience climbing mountains, let alone the tallest peak in the world, they were determined that their love was so strong it would conquer anything.

Even Mount Everest.

The air was so cold it felt angry. Pem and his bride were instructed to wear special oxygen tanks to prevent extreme altitude sickness.

The lovers' lives in this moment were held in the balance of a teetering ladder over a seemingly bottomless crevasse. At any moment loose rocks could send them plummeting, and the slippery patches of ice could spell doom if stepped on in the wrong way. Every move was critical as they continued on.

Shiesma didn't complain. Being with the love of her life was all that consumed her mind and heart. Pem, on the other hand, was, like many men, worried about his future wife making the trek safely. It was an exhausting journey, fraught with danger and close calls, but while he was concerned for his bride, he didn't allow doubt to distract him from the goal: to marry this beautiful woman and spend the rest of his life with her.

The final push to the summit would truly test their commitment. This alone took nearly thirty-six hours. But finally, through all the life-threatening steps along the way, they made it to the top. In sheer exhaustion, they pushed with all their strength to conquer the final steps of the ascent. The apex of their journey was a sight to behold—the world beneath them and a God above and all around them. The view was breathtaking and the silence deafening.

Pem and Shiesma looked at each other with a mix of emotions, their limbs trembling and their bodies desperate for rest. They had made it to their destination, and yet this was where the real journey would begin.

With extreme caution they removed their oxygen masks, exposing their tired lungs to the thin mountain air—something they had been advised not to do. They could only be exposed for a few minutes or frostbite and sickness would result.

"Pem, do you take Shiesma to be your wedded wife for better and for worse, till death do you part?"

"Yes," Pem answered with deep love in his heart.

"Shiesma, do you take Pem to be your husband, for better and for worse, till death do you part?"

"Yes," she said, with a smile that cracked her frozen lips. She fought through the pain and kissed Pem atop the mountain. Their lungs burned from the exertion, but they had managed the allotted fifteen minutes to exchange wedding vows and to make flower necklaces in accordance with their cultural customs.

The experience was nothing less than extraordinary. Here, in this moment, Pem and Shiesma became the first couple to marry on the summit of Mount Everest.

Talk about being on top of the world!

Despite all the joy they felt at that moment, the return journey still lay ahead. The descent is often when people perish.

The weather was terrible. The wind and snow mercilessly beat at their faces with such intensity that they were forced to remove their glasses just to see where they were going. But for Shiesma this didn't help.

Suddenly she started screaming, "Pem! Pem! Where are you?"

The newlywed stopped in shock at his wife's screams. He was walking right next to her, how could she not see him?

"Pem, I can't see anything!" Shiesma shouted in panic, as much as her lungs would allow it.

This is when most people would be overcome by fear. Pem, however, possessed a special gift: *relaxed intensity*.

A true leader remains calm in the midst of a storm. Like a mining foreman leading his crew in the depths of the earth, Pem remained cool under pressure.

His new wife was unaccustomed to the extreme conditions. She had become snow blind, a condition usually brought on by excessive UV rays.

Pem wondered to himself if she would ever be able to see again. "What have I done?" he thought. But he knew he needed to stay relaxed to lead them to safety.

Even though the situation was intense and frightening, he knew he couldn't overreact. He lovingly guided his wife past dangerous obstacles while whispering soothingly in her ear to keep her calm.

Eight hours later, after they had endured the harshest of elements, an overwhelming sense of relief washed over them as they approached base camp. Now that Shiesma was calmer and more protected, her eyes began to recover. She became increasingly able to make out large objects, particularly the helicopter coming in to take them down to safety.

Finally, their ordeal was over and they could begin their lives together.

And yet nothing was easy for the couple and they soon faced another challenge. Their joy for their safety quickly turned to shock and disbelief when disaster struck right before their eyes. The helicopter pilot had been struggling against the oncoming snowstorm, and was desperately attempting to keep the craft steady as strong winds rocked against the hull.

Shivering in the cold, the lovers held each other tightly as they watched a strong gust smash against the helicopter. The pilot's hand briefly slipped from the controls and the craft crashed nearby.

They could only stand in disbelief. Pem quickly realized that they would have to take decisive action. With relaxed intensity he sat his wife down and approached the wreckage to ensure that the crew had survived. He immediately smelled fuel—it had leaked all over the area. Again, Pem knew he couldn't afford to give in to fear or panic. It was vital to stay calm and collected, even under this amount of pressure.

Quickly and calmly, he helped the crew out of the wreckage and made it back to a safer area. After another long, tense period of waiting, a second helicopter eventually made it to rescue them. Finally they would be on their way.

Or would they?

The new rescue crew came down with severe altitude sickness, so the first team who had crashed had to tend to the second before they all could head down.

When Pem and his bride finally climbed into the helicopter that would take them back to safety, they held each other tightly and looked over the snowy mountaintops. They looked at each other and without saying a word they knew *their love was so strong, it would conquer anything.*

Despite all the dangers they had faced, Pem's relaxed intensity had empowered the couple to return safely. After more than sixty days enduring the grueling conditions of Mount Everest, Pem and Shiesma were finally safe and sound.

The happy couple disappeared for three years, venturing to the United States to begin their new life together. Neither of their families knew where they had gone, or even that they were married. Most assumed they had simply run away. Pem and his wife felt bad for leaving their families in the dark. After three years together, they decided to inform their relatives of their whereabouts and declare their marriage and love.

As soon as Pem's father-in-law learned that they had been married, he suffered a heart attack that sent him straight to the hospital. Pem did not find this surprising. As far as his father-in-law was concerned, they had done something so forbidden that it was unthinkable.

Pem and Shiesma knew their love would be viewed that way, but married anyway because it was what they wanted more than anything. The two were committed to climbing that mountain and getting married and nobody was going to tell them otherwise.

They had to persevere for years for the sake of their dreams, for the sake of staying true to themselves, and ultimately they knew it was worth it. Nothing could stop them. Their passion and resolve was so overwhelmingly powerful that they could literally conquer mountains.

During the quest, Pem was a shining example of *relaxed intensity*.

In life, it is inevitable that you will face obstacles and challenges. In order to overcome them, you need to stay cool, no matter how difficult this may be. Pem could not allow his own fear and doubts to affect his actions. Luis Urzúa, in Chile, could not afford to panic and lead from fear. True leaders must remain confident in spite of the circumstances around them.

Relaxed intensity allows a leader to push through hardships in a collaborative manner rather than do it alone. When a leader is relaxed, challenges are handled effectively. Think about it: would you follow someone who panics and shows nothing but fear?

Likely not. We tend to follow those who appear unruffled when faced with tough situations. These individuals project the confidence that they have what it takes to overcome the challenge.

And they are no different from you!

Have you ever wondered if you have what it takes to be a great leader?

Simply put: You do!

We all do!

Nobody is born a leader, and yet everyone is born with leadership potential.

Leadership, in other words, is *learned* and *practiced*. Above all else, leaders are those who learn how to convert fear into relaxed intensity. This is not an intrinsic or natural process—where some *have it* and some don't. It takes conscious practice to summon the latent potential with which we are all endowed.

Think of *potential* simply as our ability to learn—from mistakes. Like Luis Urzúa and Pem, we must learn to control our fear if we want to lead ourselves and others.

A true leader rises above the crowd to become someone special. Leaders are not afraid to step up and stand out, and have the courage to take the role.

HOW CAN YOU DEVELOP RELAXED INTENSITY AND HANDLE CHALLENGES EFFECTIVELY?

Stay true to yourself.

LET YOUR passion and commitment become stronger than your fears. Remember the examples of Luis and

Pem. The challenges they faced could not stop them, because they knew endurance was worth it. Instead of focusing on your challenges along the way, always focus on your outcome.

Don't try to blend in out of fear of being different.

UNDERSTAND that it is your job as a great leader to stand out and take the lead. Sometimes this means acting against the status quo. It is easy to blend in, but oftentimes this can be dangerous when change is needed.

Know that you have what it takes to be a great leader.

LEADERSHIP is not reserved for a special few who are somehow born with superhuman qualities. Leadership is *learned*. This means we are all capable of being great leaders. This also means we must learn how to face challenges with composure and poise. Only then will we clearly see the solutions necessary to achieving our goals.

CHAPTER 4

Defining Your Cul-de-Sac Moments

——— ✤ ———

"*LIGHTS! CAMERA! ACTION!*"

Gary W. Goldstein loved the movie industry more than anything. He knew when he started his career that the odds of making it big were rivaled only by those of the lottery. Every year, tens of thousands of fresh new faces come to Los Angeles with the dream of becoming the next great film actor, screenwriter, or director, and breaking into the Hollywood elite.

The movie industry is not for the faint of heart or for those who expect things to come easy.

For Gary, producing films such as *Ringmaster*, *Under Siege* and *Under Siege 2*, and a lesser-known project called *Cannibal Women in the Avocado Jungle of Death*, had required years of hard work and, of course, *stickability*. But it was a script titled *3,000* that would be the cornerstone of Gary's career as a producer.

Fast forward . . .

As Gary watched Julia Roberts receive the Academy Award for Best Actress in 2001, his thoughts wandered to the day he first saw her. One of Gary's director friends had invited him to screen a movie. It is very common for industry folks to get together and give one another feedback before a movie goes into final production. It was a rainy day and although he didn't feel like going, he didn't want to let his friend down, so he pulled himself up by his bootstraps and went.

Looking back, he's happy he did. The young actress had impressed him—first on the screen and even more so in person when they had lunch together a few weeks later. There was something about her—she had an incredible personality and charisma, and embodied what's known as the X-factor in the industry.

A miraculous combination of events had led to his most iconic film. Gary smiled as he remembered how his most popular film came to be.

Many years earlier, he needed somebody to help him with his computer. This was back when you needed a professional programmer because there was no way you could figure it out on your own. A friend had recommended a programmer named

Daniel, so Gary called him. He discovered that Daniel had written a script, which was no surprise—in Hollywood just about everyone has "the next best script" ready under their arm. Gary offered to read it, expecting that it would be the same as the hundreds of other scripts he had seen (and turned down) over the years.

But this one, called *3,000*, was different. It was actually very good. Daniel was excited, and was more than willing to make the improvements Gary suggested. They found an agent, but studio after studio refused the script. Daniel's hope was fading, yet Gary refused to give up.

"Daniel," Gary said. "Once you know you are on to something special, never—and I mean never—let someone else talk you out of your dream."

Three weeks later they had a meeting with Disney. Most of the other studios had already turned them down, so they had decided to give it a shot.

"Well," one of the executives spoke up. "We like the script, but can you make it more Disney-esque? Currently, it's a four out of ten on the Disney likeability factor, and we need it to be a seven. Can you do this?"

Rubbing his chin, Gary paused for a moment. The room fell into an uncomfortable silence. Looking up to the ceiling, Gary made a few *hmmmmm* sounds as he took off his glasses to clean them. The executives held their breaths in anticipation, wondering what was taking so long, when Gary finally spoke up.

"Absolutely!" Gary responded. "No problem. We can do that! Let's work out the details."

As they left the building, Gary could hardly contain his excitement, and yet Daniel didn't look happy at all.

"Gary?" Daniel said carefully, so no one could hear. "What do they mean by making the script more Disney-like?"

With a devilish grin from ear to ear, Gary whispered back, "I have no idea, but you will have your first movie!"

"What?" Daniel asked, confused. "You don't know what they mean, yet you told them I can rewrite the script?"

Gary laughs every time he thinks about it. "You say *yes* and *then* you make it happen. We'll figure it out as we go! Let's celebrate our success!"

In order to make the script more Disney-like, one of the things that needed changing was the title—*3,000*, the amount of money the leading lady charged for a date, would not suit Disney. What would be a more apt title?

Pretty Woman.

And the rest is history.

Can you imagine, pitching a romantic love story about a virginal prostitute to Disney?

While Gary enjoyed being part of that historic project, his

favorite movie that he produced was called *The Mothman Prophecies*, which also starred Richard Gere.

Convincing Disney had been a breeze compared to the challenge of finding a home for this one.

The studios unanimously agreed: *Great script, great casting. Thank you for sending it over. It's going to be a pass.*

Only one studio remained that hadn't read the script. When they called Gary to tell him they were not going to produce it either, his heart sank.

They too said, "It's great, we love it, wonderful idea. We are going to pass."

This seemed to be the end of the road. Only this call was different. Gary felt something, and asked for a meeting with the executive team.

Based on his personal relationship with them, they were happy to grant the request. But during their meeting they repeated the same message: "Great story, and after talking for a little while—we need to tell you, again, face-to-face, Gary. It's going to be a pass for us."

After another one of his (now famous) momentary pauses, Gary answered calmly with the only appropriate response he could come up with: "Thank you, but I respectfully *pass* on your pass."

The room went silent.

Gary wasn't nervous. He wasn't upset. He was dead serious, and they could tell.

"You do what?" one of them asked. "What do you mean?"

"I respectfully pass on your pass," Gary responded with conviction. "The reason I am so adamant about seeing this come to life is that the story reminds me of the deep relationship I had with my father. After his death I suffered the intense pain of losing a loved one, just like the main character in the script does. This is no longer about business. It has become personal. Everybody can relate to the feeling that your heart is being ripped apart, because they have been through it or know somebody who has."

As he continued, the executives' perspective on the script changed as they were touched by Gary's genuine emotions. Based on this meeting, they unanimously agreed to produce the film.

For Gary this was a *cul-de-sac moment*—a time in your life where you go inside and set up shop, or simply choose to drive on past. In a cul-de-sac there is no exit. There is no retreat. Once you commit to venturing forward, you must live with the consequences.

Goldstein knew that he could try to push past their *no* and make an effort to convince them, or he could turn around and walk away, even though there was nowhere else to go. His willingness to stand his ground and speak openly showed them that they were about to turn down something special, which changed their attitude and created a Hollywood success story.

In life, we have to define our cul-de-sac moments. Truth is, there are moments that we have to accept not having something. There are also moments when, in order to succeed, we have to be willing to break through the thick wall of rejection in our path.

We may even need to "pass on a pass" from time to time.

Speaking in a louder-than-normal voice, Gary insisted, "Many people give up too quickly and don't have the *stickability* to succeed."

It's not strange that many people are afraid to hear "no." From the time we were born, we spoke up whenever we wanted or needed something. There was no buffer, and we knew no words. As we learned to speak, though, we heard "no" more than anything else.

It has been estimated that a toddler hears "no" an astonishing four hundred times a day, and forty thousand times by the age of five. Conversely, they hear "yes" only five thousand times. Consider this! We begin our lives experiencing a negative response eight times more often than a positive response.

We tend to see what we are looking for and hear what we want to hear.

—⁓⁓⁓—

Flashback . . .

Remember being wheeled around in a grocery cart at the store as a kid? You asked for anything and everything you laid your eyes on—from toys to sugar-filled boxes of happiness. Maybe you even reached out and grabbed items from the shelf, while your parent swiped at your arms like lion tamers to keep you inside the boundaries of your metal cage.

"No, no, no."

How many times have we heard this in the grocery store or elsewhere? With this much *doubt training*, it's little wonder that so many great people are afraid to allow themselves to do something great. There's nothing more common than unsuccessful people with talent. These are the folks who fail not because they inherently lack something, but because self-doubt prevents them from overcoming obstacles. These are the people who end up passing up golden opportunities.

How many opportunities have slipped through our fingers because of doubt, the fear of failing, or being told "no"?

The possibility of success lies in a single word: faith. Faith in our spirit, our talents, and even a higher power.

Which brings us to Leah O'Brien-Amico, a living example of what is possible when you have faith and are committed to be your best in everything you do. You may know her as the three-time Olympic gold-medal winner in women's softball.

Leah is also a wonderful wife, mother of three beautiful children, TV host, speaker, teacher, and trainer. Her faith is the foundation that creates balance in her life, and that is where true success and happiness comes from.

Leah has been an inspiration to other athletes by showing them that it is possible to have it all. She demonstrated this by showing her teammates that it's okay to be a great competitor, a great wife, and a great mother—she was the only mom on the 2004 Olympic team.

She did this by having the faith that she could truly have it all.

In a one-on-one meeting, Leah said, "Every role requires a *winner's mind-set* in its own way. So many people think they can multitask, but the reality is that you miss out if you do. When I am with my kids I am fully present and one hundred percent focused on being the best mom I can be."

When she goes out to speak, Leah switches and becomes the best teacher she can be. The key to her success has been her ability to be focused and fully present with one thing at a time.

In the digital age of constant stimuli and multitasking, *focus* is quickly becoming a lost art. For Leah, this is a shame. We must be the best we can be in everything we do. This is not easy, of course, and this is our challenge. Those of us willing to apply the necessary balance of *stickability* and *flexibility* to achieve our goals shall reap the benefits we seek.

As an athlete, Leah learned to be flexible and go with the flow, regardless of what life threw at her.

She asks rhetorically, "How do you respond to adversity? Are you going to fight back, or give up?"

We are all faced with this challenge—you are not alone!

Leah speaks from experience when she shares, "Adversity will reveal your true character. Anybody can go out, win, and have a big smile on his face. The question is: what do you do when things get hard? Your faith needs to be strongest when you are dealing with challenges. Faith can help you to accept that you can only control the controllable. It also helps to keep things in the right order of importance."

How does she apply her faith?

By surrounding herself with people who encourage her to keep pressing on and stay focused on her goal. As an athlete she knows the importance of having a team.

She explains, "In life there are things we will go through. You need a team around you, just like in sports. Even athletes who don't compete in a team activity have a team to support them. There are times when I'm down and they encourage me, other times, it's the other way around."

This is true in athletics, business, and every area of life. People on top leave negativity behind. When you walk away from people with negative attitudes, it doesn't mean you hate them, it just means you like yourself more.

We all need support in our lives. If ever you find yourself without mentors around you, remember the Buddhist proverb: "When the student is ready, the teacher will appear."

Leah continued, "There are people around us who are willing to help, but you need to voice it. You need to voice what you want. Sometimes it's all we need, that little push. Ask for it!

"When I started out, my goal was to be an Olympic gold medalist. There was nothing less. It was all about the end result. There was a big picture at the end of the day. The focus was that gold medal. You can't slack off one day. Ultimately I knew that I had to do the workout and training required— whether it was lifting weights, running, conditioning, whatever. If we had workouts, inside of me I was not okay with doing anything less than giving it my all. I would show up early and leave late. You need to set a higher standard to be the best you can be, no matter what you are doing. You can't give a half-hearted effort and expect to be successful."

Leah understood the Napoleon Hill success formula. She took the four simple yet necessary steps that gave her the *stickability* to achieve the goal of becoming an Olympic gold medalist.

A definite purpose backed by a burning desire for its fulfillment.

LEAH WAS crystal clear on her purpose. Her goal was not just to participate in the Olympics. She was determined to be an Olympic gold medalist.

A definite plan, expressed by continuous action.

LEAH HAD a training schedule and she executed it diligently. The work she did every single day built her confidence. Every time she stepped on the field she worked on her weaknesses to become better, while at the same time fortifying her strengths.

A mind closed tightly against all negative and discouraging influences, including negative suggestions of relatives, friends, and acquaintances.

LEAH DIDN'T allow negative people around her. She did not accept any negativity, not even from her own teammates. You have to protect your mind and how you are responding to your thoughts, because the words that you speak on the inside will eventually manifest on the outside.

A friendly alliance with one person (or more) that will encourage one to follow through with both plan and purpose.

LEAH HAD a great support team built around her— her parents, the senior softball players in college, her Olympic teammates, and others who believed in her and pulled her through the difficult times.

"Don't give up on your dream," Leah declares passionately. "Even if you feel you want to quit. Hang on a little bit longer. Be the best in everything you do. Step out of your comfort zone. That is often when miracles happen."

The fact of the matter is that most successful people don't just have success fall into their laps. It was focus, faith, *stickability*, and hours and hours of training that made Leah an Olympic gold medalist—three times!

She embodies a lesson found in this great quote from Ralph Waldo Emerson:

Self-trust is the first secret of success.

You have to make it happen even if the odds are against you, even if others tell you, "You can't do it," or "We're going to take a pass." Many people we think of as successful have achieved only because they had the *stickability* to persist despite rejection. They struggled onward to meet their goal because they wouldn't take "no" for an answer.

Author J. K. Rowling, best known for the megahit Harry Potter series, had to struggle for quite some time before she found success. Before she was published, she was a divorced, nearly penniless single mother who suffered from depression. Rowling had to depend on welfare while attending school, writing, and raising her child. On top of all that, twelve different publishers rejected her first Harry Potter book before she found the one that gave it a chance. She didn't allow her circumstances or her multiple rejection letters to keep her down. Through hard work and *stickability*, she went from living on welfare to being one of the richest women in the world in the span of only five years!

The very first time comedian Jerry Seinfeld stepped on stage at a comedy club, he looked out at the audience and froze up until he was driven from the stage by the boos and jeers of the crowd. This didn't stop him from pursuing a career as a stand-up comic. Now, he is the beloved comedic champion we all know.

None of these people allowed rejection to keep them down. They simply kept going and eventually broke through to greatness. They didn't let the pain of failure prevent them from sticking with their goals.

What sometimes holds us back the most isn't the sting of failure, but rather the expectations of others. Whether family, friends, or relative strangers, others have expectations for what you will become. If your own expectations conflict with theirs it can cause tensions. Sometimes, we get so caught up in what other people think of us that we're afraid to put ourselves out there.

We lose our faith.

We begin to listen to those voices, the ones that tell us that we shouldn't follow our dreams because of this or that reason, and before we know it, we've given up on what we want to do. Are we willing to push through despite any criticism we may receive? Many of the greatest minds the world has ever known had to struggle with this very obstacle. Their examples can serve as an inspiration to us all.

Life is hard when we are filled with self-induced doubt, let alone when outside sources pile on top of it. Note that these are *outside* forces! We must have deep faith from *within* to combat negativity. Never let another person talk you out of what you want to be and do. If you do, you may never realize what kind of impact you could have on the world.

Have faith to persist because only *you* know what you're capable of—and then *you* shall be an incredible inspiration to others.

—⁓—

HOW CAN YOU FIND A WAY TO BREAK THROUGH AND ACHIEVE YOUR PERSONAL GREATNESS?

Pass on the pass.

UNDERSTAND and accept that success often lies behind a thick wall of rejection. Don't let that stop you. When you know you are on to something special, you have to stand your ground.

Apply Napoleon Hill's four steps to develop stickability.

HAVE a definite purpose, take continuous action on your plan, close your mind tightly against all negativity, and surround yourself with supportive people.

Fake it till you make it!

SEE YOURSELF already as the best person you can be. Create pictures in your imagination of what you want to achieve. Visualize your goal to every last detail and you will be able to clearly define your cul-de-sac moments.

CHAPTER 5

Above the Line of Super-Credibility

———❦———

PETER DIAMANDIS STEPPED ONTO THE STAGE. HIS HEART was beating through his chest as the spotlight hit his face. This was the moment he had been waiting for. He knew he had to take advantage of this unique opportunity to realize his vision: launching a private, reusable manned craft into space.

There he was in St. Louis, Missouri, sharing the stage with famous astronauts, the Lindbergh family, the head of the National Aeronautics and Space Administration (NASA), and the head of the Federal Aviation Administration (FAA). Peter understood the power of incentive pricing (offering a reward in return for accomplishment), and he knew that St. Louis was the place to be.

It all began in 1919. Raymond Orteig, a Frenchman who

owned the Brevoort and Lafayette hotels in New York City, made the flying world an extraordinary offer. He would award $25,000 to the first aviator to fly nonstop between New York and Paris. It was this challenge that encouraged the people of St. Louis to fund Charles Lindbergh to build the aircraft that made him an overnight aviation icon and allowed him to win the $25,000 prize in May 1927 (for context, $25,000 in 1927 would be equivalent to almost $325,000 today). You may remember this from history class as the *Spirit of St. Louis.*

Peter's passion and commitment had inspired about a hundred people of various backgrounds from St. Louis to give him a couple million dollars, which he called the "New Spirit of St. Louis."

Just as Charles Lindbergh had been full of confidence when his team was building his airplane, Peter possessed unshakable faith that it was possible for a nongovernmental organization to build a spacecraft that could climb to 100 kilometers above the earth. He knew that the world's most precious resource is a passionate and committed human mind.

The question was, could he convince others to share his vision?

At the right moment, Peter took the microphone and announced, "Ladies and gentleman, in this time and age, nothing is impossible."

He continued, "Technology has advanced more in the last decade than in the hundred years before. The resources are available and the human mind is capable of achieving more than ever before. Charles Lindbergh impacted our world forever and we are on the bridge of the next historic moment. Very soon the first private spaceship will go into space.

"The person who will build this first spaceship that can go one hundred kilometers into space with multiple passengers, return safely to Earth, and repeat the process will win the X Prize of ten million dollars!"

A huge applause erupted. Media all over the world picked up the news: a $10 million prize for whoever could build the first private reusable spaceship.

Who dared to question Peter Diamandis as he stood next to the Lindbergh family, the head of NASA, the head of the FAA, and twenty astronauts? Who would have ever suspected that Peter did not have anywhere near $10 million to give to the winner of the competition?

Peter's action was brilliant!

He stood above the line of credibility when he made this impactful, bold announcement. You see, when you are *under* the line of credibility, people dismiss you immediately and don't take you seriously. Above the line of credibility, you are given a chance to prove yourself, and your words are believed without a shadow of a doubt. In this case, Peter took advantage of the power of association by borrowing the fame and success of the others who graced the stage. This supercharged his credibility.

One of Peter's laws of success is: "The best way to predict the future is to create it yourself!" And that is exactly what he did.

Once he got people to buy into his dream, it was time for the next step: finding more sponsors to put up the $10 million. He figured they would be eager to be part of something so historic. He called the billionaire Sir Richard Branson, founder of the Virgin Group, but to Peter's surprise Sir Richard wasn't interested in getting involved. He shook his head and asked, "Can somebody really do this?"

"Of course!" Peter answered. "We are about to change the world. If it were easy it would have been done already, but that doesn't mean it can't be done. The day before a breakthrough, it's always considered a crazy idea."

He couldn't convince Sir Richard, but that didn't stop him. He went to person after person, corporation after corporation, pitching his vision to hundreds of CEOs, with no takers.

"Somebody may die trying," they spouted, believing the risk to be too high.

Peter started to get a little worried. How in the world

would he raise $10 million if people couldn't see his vision? Where would he find sponsors for the X Prize if hundreds of CEOs had already turned him down?

Announcing the competition had been a thrilling experience. He had been confident that it would be easy to raise the money. It blew his mind that they didn't want to be involved in changing the future of humanity.

There were already twenty-six teams participating in the competition. They took Peter at his word and were hard at work, planning and creating new spacecrafts to accomplish the challenge before them. Peter didn't want to let them down. He didn't want to admit defeat. His reputation was on the line, not to mention his dream.

Peter reminded himself of one of his own laws of success:

If you think it is impossible, then it is . . . for you.

If he gave up at this point, his aspiration would never be realized. What's more, everything he believed in, everything he stood for, would crumble.

Giving up was not an option.

Instead of fixating on the considerable obstacles he faced, Peter focused intensely on a solution. Day and night he wracked his brain and considered all possible resources.

And then: an epiphany!

He found an insurance company that was willing to sell him a "hole-in-one policy." This kind of insurance is very common in funding big prizes for golf matches. If somebody makes a hole in one and is entitled to a large sum of money, the insurance company provides the money for the prize and the organizer only has to pay the premium. This is a safe bet as the chances of a hole in one are very slim. The risk is very low for the insurance company.

In Peter's case, the insurance company determined that the premium for the $10 million X Prize would be $3 million, paid up front.

The insurance company considered this free money. They had hired a consultant to speak with the major players in aeronautics—companies like Boeing and Lockheed Martin— to gauge the likelihood of somebody actually succeeding. Experts at these companies told the consultant it was impossible. They didn't have the faith that anyone could accomplish this task, not even themselves—they would not even bother competing. Thinking that it was a safe bet, the insurance company offered Peter the hole-in-one insurance.

With the policy in place, Peter was faced with his next challenge. He had already used the money from the St. Louis benefactors and had nothing left to pay for the policy. After negotiations, the insurance company agreed to accept $50,000 per month, with the balance due in a single payment at the end of the year. But this didn't help. After only a few months Peter's resources were exhausted. He was out of capital.

Just imagine what was at stake! If he did not come up with $50,000 every month, the policy would be defunct and he would lose everything.

Peter searched for the money as relentlessly as a man searches for air while submerged underwater. Each month, he feared "50K Friday," when the insurance company expected payment. Raising capital became his defined purpose. With passion, commitment, and confidence, he poured his soul into finding sponsors who believed in the X Prize.

He refused to let rejection after rejection stop him, and resolved to reinterpret what "no" meant—for him. Instead of rejection, he decided "no" simply meant: *begin again at one level higher.*

A number of people on his board had even stepped in to help him out, but their resources were reaching their limit as another 50K Friday approached. It was already Tuesday and Peter felt like his back was against a wall.

After a sleepless night, he desperately needed coffee. He went to a little shop around the corner from his house and ordered his favorite: a cinnamon latte with extra whipped cream.

With the warm drink in hand, he took his usual seat near the window.

It was at this moment that everything changed.

Pulling a *Forbes* magazine out of his worn briefcase, he read about an Iranian woman who had just sold her company. In the article she was listed as one of the "Wealthiest 40 under 40."

His heart skipped a beat and a big smile appeared on his face. His eye caught a line in her bio that would become the biggest game-changer ever. In clear black type, it said that her dream was to fly on a suborbital flight into space.

He couldn't believe it.

Whatever you seek is also seeking you.

Peter knew immediately that he had found someone who would be willing to help him, and in the process he would be helping her to achieve *her* dream.

The woman was Anousheh Ansari.

As a young girl, Anousheh had dreamed about space. More than anything, she wanted to be able to travel to the stars one day. Realistically, however, growing up as a female in Iran, she knew her chances of ever seeing her dream come true were slim to none.

In Iran, women are viewed by many as physically, emotionally, and mentally inferior to men, and are forced to live under a brutal system of gender apartheid. Many are considered the property of men and must get permission from them to engage in many activities we take for granted, such as attending school or finding employment.

Truth is, many Iranian women spend their whole lives in isolation, being allowed to associate only with their immediate family. For Anousheh, traveling to space was as far-fetched as any fantasy one could imagine. But unlike most Iranian women with big dreams, this young woman was given a unique opportunity.

When she was only fifteen, after the Islamic Revolution, she and her family moved to the United States, where she was no longer restricted by the oppressive circumstances she was accustomed to.

She didn't speak English and arrived in a country that was very different from everything she had known. But she didn't let this hold her back. She took advantage of the freedom to finally develop her potential by earning a bachelor's degree in electronics and computer engineering from George Mason University. She went on to earn a master's degree in electrical engineering from George Washington University, which eventually led to an honorary doctorate from the International Space University.

Over time, she successfully built and sold multiple businesses. Once her confidence was proven and developed, she did exactly what Leah O'Brien advised in the previous chapter: "You need to voice what you want."

State it and create it.

In her *Forbes* magazine bio, Anousheh divulged that it was her dream to travel through space. She didn't know that there was somebody out there who wanted to help her achieve that dream. If she had never stated it, he would never have known.

When Peter and Anousheh got together, she immediately agreed to help fund his project. With the money the Ansari family contributed, Peter was able to pay for the hole-in-one insurance policy and the expenses of the foundation.

As a gesture of gratitude, the contest was renamed the Ansari X Prize. With funding in place and focus redirected toward the goal, groups began testing their crafts.

When somebody *almost* succeeded, the insurance company called Peter. He was excited, because he expected they wanted to get involved. "Maybe they want to become a sponsor," he thought to himself.

Instead, they offered him $5 million to cancel the deal. They knew that folks were on the brink of success and wanted out to save themselves a huge loss.

Of course, there was no way Peter was willing to cancel the contest.

On October 4, 2004, Mojave Aerospace Ventures (MAV) won the Ansari X Prize with their craft *SpaceShipOne*. They were the first team to build and fly a three-passenger vehicle 100 kilometers into space—twice within two weeks! The insurance company paid out the $10 million as agreed.

A couple of years later, on September 18, 2006, Anousheh Ansari captured headlines of her own when she became the first female private space explorer. She earned a place in history as the fourth private explorer to visit space and the first astronaut of Iranian descent.

To get what you want, simply help others get what they want.

There had been many times Peter could have given up along the way, but his faith pushed him forward in spite of all odds and motivated him to do things that nobody else even thought possible.

In persevering, he created a movement that changed the world.

He had a vision and would not allow anyone or anything stop him from realizing it. He experienced firsthand that *patience is a virtue, but persistence to the point of success is a blessing.*

Just like Peter Diamandis, Anousheh Ansari held on to her vision even when the odds were against her. Her *stickability* led to spending eleven glorious days in space.

As she describes it, "I saw Earth as a beautiful blue ball in the darkness of space and felt its warmth and energy. Let me tell you . . . there is nothing like it. From up there you see one Earth, one home for all of us. The only thing separating us from each other is water and the only thing keeping us from instant death is that thin glowing blue atmosphere that surrounds us. When you look at Earth from up there, you have a new perspective. You can see how insignificant we are compared to the universe that surrounds us. It is an empowering experience because everything seems so small. You feel like anything is possible and changing the world does not seem like such a daunting task."

What would our lives be like if we could go beyond what is perceived to be possible?

Consider that what is *possible* and what is *impossible* is largely a matter of *perception*. This means it is up to us to determine what we can and cannot do. Think of it this way: your perception is just as valuable and real as anyone else's.

Peter and Anousheh were able to redefine what is possible. And they are no different from any of us! Peter's perception of what is possible went beyond the norm, and now the norm is what he perceived. Even Sir Richard Branson (yes, the same man who turned Peter down at the beginning of the story!) is now building his own space tourism business, called Virgin Galactic. He ended up licensing the rights for the X-Prize–winning spacecraft design, and Virgin Galactic is now considered the leader in the budding space tourism industry that Peter and Anousheh helped create. Better late than never!

WHAT LESSONS CAN WE DRAW FROM THESE STORIES?

Exceed the line of super-credibility.

WHEN YOU surround yourself with successful people, you get to borrow their credibility. Others will take you seriously and won't question you, because you are above the line of super-credibility. Even when we doubt ourselves, sometimes we take ease in knowing that others believe in us more than we do.

Set yourself up to succeed.

PETER DIDN'T say, "I'm raising money to give away this prize" or "My goal is to raise $10 million." By beginning the project before he had raised all the prize money, he set himself up so he *had* to succeed no matter the obstacles. When you voice your vision aloud, others can step in to help you achieve it, as was the case for Anousheh.

When in doubt: THINK!

DON'T GIVE UP when people throw obstacles in your path because they don't believe your vision is possible. Devise creative ways to find solutions, and find the people who share your vision and are excited to help you achieve it.

There were moments when Peter's doubts might have distracted him from his goal. But he did not allow those fears to overtake his faith. Napoleon Hill refers to these demons as "ghosts of fear." Before we examine these in the next chapter, let's review Peter's laws of success. Hanging on the wall of his office, these time-tested principles guide him in all aspects of his illustrious life.

PETER'S LAWS
The Creed of the Persistent and Passionate Mind

1. If anything can go wrong, fix it! (To hell with Murphy!)
2. When given a choice . . . take both!
3. Multiple projects lead to multiple successes.
4. Start at the top, then work your way up.

5. Do it by the book . . . but be the author!

6. When forced to compromise, ask for more.

7. If it's worth doing, it's got to be done right now.

8. If you can't win, change the rules.

9. If you can't change the rules, then ignore them.

10. Perfection is not optional.

11. When faced without a challenge, make one.

12. "No" simply means begin again at one level higher.

13. Don't walk when you can run.

14. Bureaucracy is a challenge to be conquered with a righteous attitude, a tolerance for stupidity, and a bulldozer when necessary.

15. When in doubt: THINK!

16. Patience is a virtue, but persistence to the point of success is a blessing.

17. The squeaky wheel gets replaced.

18. The faster you move, the slower time passes, the longer you live.

19. The best way to predict the future is to create it yourself!

20. The ratio of something to nothing is infinite.

21. You get what you incentivize.

22. If you think it is impossible, then it is . . . for you.

23. An expert is someone who can tell you exactly how it can't be done.

24. The day before something is a breakthrough, it's a crazy idea.

25. If it were easy, it would have been done already.

26. Without a target you'll miss it every time.

27. Bullshit walks, hardware talks.

28. A crisis is a terrible thing to waste.

29. The world's most precious resource is the passionate and committed human mind.

30. If you can't measure it, you can't improve it.

CHAPTER 6

Overcoming the Ghosts of Fear

MANY PEOPLE HAVE BIG DREAMS AND GREAT IDEAS, BUT why do only so few take action and have the *stickability* to succeed?

Fear.

Fear can halt expansion and development. Fear can prevent true success from being achieved. Fear can become your biggest enemy. If you let it.

In Napoleon Hill's classics, *Think and Grow Rich* and *Outwitting the Devil*, the author does a tremendous job of casting a spotlight on the number one reason most people give up—so much so that he dedicated the longest chapter to this topic.

Sharon Lechter—coauthor of The Napoleon Hill Foundation's national bestseller *Three Feet from Gold*, and coauthor of the international bestseller *Rich Dad, Poor Dad*—was given a copy of the seventy-five-year-old hidden manuscript titled *Outwitting the Devil* and read it one night. In an interview, she reminded us not to be afraid of the *devil* concept: "Do not let the name 'devil' do the devil's work."

"The essence of the book is to learn how to drive negativity out of your life," Sharon continued, speaking of *Outwitting the Devil*. "Hill teaches us that the way to do this is to have faith in a higher power, and in you. This is the only way to overcome the demon that holds us back by fear."

Recognizing fear is empowering. But what is fear, and why does it play such a major role in causing people to give up? According to the dictionary definition, fear is "a distressing emotion aroused by impending danger, evil, pain, etc., whether the threat is real or imagined." Yes, in many cases the threat exists only in your imagination, but still it has a powerful effect.

The stronger the vibration of fear within us, the more it governs our thoughts in a negative way. We know that thoughts control what we do. Just imagine how empowered you will be when the vibrations of success are stronger than those of fear.

Hill's research shows that people can do tremendous things and attain all they want in life if they can conquer the obstacles related to fear. On the other hand, if we allow fear to control us, it can stop us dead in our tracks.

"Fear is inside of us and it can paralyze us," Sharon believes. "*Stickability* is to know that what you're doing is right and keep going. It's knowing what you want and being absolutely destined to get there."

Having a map, after all, will not do you any good if you don't know where you are or where you want to go. *Stickability* helps you recalibrate and get back on track to achieve your major definite purpose.

"We all get off course," Sharon reassured. "When I get off course I go back to my passion, which is my starting point, or point of departure toward any goal."

Passion can originate from a number of emotions. For example: "Why don't we teach children about money and ethics in school?" Sharon asked. Her advocacy for financial literacy education is based on a more fundamental passion for helping people.

"Every night before bed, my father asked me, 'Have you made a difference in somebody's life today?' And now every night before I go to bed I ask myself the same question."

This practice broadens Sharon's perspective on what is possible. "So many of us wait for the answer to the question 'Why?'" Sharon explained. "Instead, ask 'Why not?' and you'll be able to step into the unknown with confidence and success. When we review all the fears Napoleon Hill lays out in his work, I think that one of the most detrimental is the fear of change, or what I refer to as the fear of the unknown. The more educated we are, the more willing we are to accept the unknown, and the more likely we will overcome the most universal of all fears."

Hill explains in his teachings that there are six primary forces that hold us back from our greatest dreams and desires. He calls them the "Six Ghosts of Fear." He lists these barriers as:

1. The Fear of Poverty
2. The Fear of Criticism
3. The Fear of Ill Health
4. The Fear of Loss of Love
5. The Fear of Old Age
6. The Fear of Death

Let's examine each in more detail.

———

The Fear of Poverty

Hill begins with what he claims is the most destructive fear. "Fear of poverty is a state of mind, nothing else! This fear paralyzes the faculty of reason, destroys imagination, kills off self-reliance, undermines enthusiasm, discourages initiative, leads to uncertainty of purpose, encourages procrastination, wipes out enthusiasm, and makes self-control an impossibility."

Fear of poverty can have quite a bit of power if you allow it. Once you understand that it is a state of mind, you can *decide* to change it. The fear of poverty basically kills all qualities and attributes needed to succeed. Without reason, imagination, self-reliance, enthusiasm, and initiative, you won't be able to achieve much. In order to be successful, you need certainty of purpose, and to take action.

The more you focus on this fear, the more likely you are to struggle financially. Hill determined that people tend to attract exactly what they focus on. Those who are financially secure see themselves as such, while those who struggle accept that as their destiny.

Once you realize that fear of poverty is a state of mind and that you will attract what you focus on, you can consciously direct your thoughts to overcome this fear. See yourself as financially secure instead of losing yourself in a stack of bills. Move through your fear by taking action and increasing your success vibration.

The Fear of Criticism

You have this great idea and can't wait to tell your friends and family about it. Unfortunately, they don't share your excitement and give you a million reasons why it won't work and why you can't do it. Before you know it, you start to doubt yourself and agree that it was a stupid idea.

As the great author explains, criticism is the "one form of service, which everyone gives too much. Everyone has a stockpile of it which is handed out, gratis (free), whether called for or not." Also, Hill observes, "One's nearest relatives are often the worst offenders."

For some reason, what people think of us becomes a factor in our achievement. It can have such an impact that, unfortunately, many a soul has been limited by other people's opinions. But that is all they are—somebody's opinions. You have to decide who you want to be in control of your thoughts and life. You or others?

They say public speaking is universally the greatest fear. Why? The only logical reason would be the fear of being criticized by our audience. So many of us never bother to develop the skills that would help us overcome this fear and enjoy speaking in front of others on topics we are passionate about.

Great public speakers have to work hard at honing their craft. The first step is to overcome the fear of what others might think of us.

Imagine walking down the street in a city you have never visited before. You trip over your loose shoelaces and catch yourself. What is the *first* thing you do? You look around to determine who saw you, right? Even though you don't know a single person in that city, your initial reaction is to see who witnessed the faux pas—always questioning, "Who was watching me?" and even more importantly, "What are they thinking?"

The Fear of Ill Health

The next shackle Hill lists in his final chapter is the fear of ill health. It doesn't take a rocket scientist to see how "certain unethical people have engaged in the business of [selling health] by keeping this fear alive," as Hill wrote more than eighty years ago.

When you watch the evening news, commercial after commercial will tell you about the latest ailment for which you need medication. And, although the side effects of the newly suggested drug may be greater than the problem you didn't know you had in the first place, people run out in droves to gain access to the latest miracle cure. By taking advantage of the fear of ill health, they cause people to focus on an illness they may or may not have and spend money on something they may not even need.

Again, the fear is created in the mind. As Hill often notes, these thoughts are driven by what we focus on—in this case, fear of an illness we may never get. Once you learn how to take control of your own thoughts, overcoming this fear won't be difficult. Of course, you want to take good care of your body and stay in shape, but you don't want the fear of ill health to dominate your thinking.

The Fear of Loss of Love

The next fear Hill illustrates is the loss of love—the most painful of all fears. Hill says, "It probably plays more havoc with the body and mind than the others, and probably stems from the Stone Age, when men stole women by brute force. Currently, this is continually practiced, yet the technique has changed. Now they use persuasion, fine cars, and other 'bait' to lure their desire."

The distinguishing symptoms of this fear are:

Jealousy. Being suspicious of friends and loved ones without reasonable evidence or sufficient cause.

Fault-finding. Looking for faults in others upon the slightest provocation.

Gambling. The habit of taking hazardous chances to provide money for loved ones with the belief that love can be purchased.

The Fear of Old Age

Fear of old age is innately built into our psyche from early on, according to Hill. Why are people afraid of getting old? "This grows from two sources. First, the thought that old age may bring with it poverty. Secondly, and by far the most common source, from false and cruel teachings of the past, which have been too well mixed with fire and brimstone and other bogies, cunningly designed to enslave man through fear."

The second source is pretty self-explanatory, so let's examine Hill's first point. No one wants to end up in the "poor house." This is why so much attention is placed on retirement programs, social security, and the like.

Every trained insurance agent or financial planner is taught to share this one line with every potential client: "For your family's sake, and to avoid putting any extra burden upon them, I just want to help your money last as long as you do."

This is designed, again, to place fear into the prospective client. And this brings us to the final major cause of fear: death.

The Fear of Death

The fear of death can be the cruelest of all, because rather than making the most out of life, the focus is on dying. This is usually caused by a lack of purpose in life. Statistics show that people tend to die not long after their retirement if they don't find another purpose in life.

Having a definite major purpose is the single greatest driver toward living a fulfilling life. The more we feel we add value, the more we tend to ensure our longevity. The more we feel our life has meaning, the richer our life will be and the longer we'll want to live.

In order to succeed, it is critical that you get rid of fear—all of the fears. This is a challenge. It requires that you master your thoughts rather than allowing your thoughts to master you. Your mind will create reality out of your fear-driven thoughts, just as readily as it will create reality out of the thoughts that are based on courage and faith. When you fill your mind with doubt and fear, your fears become your reality. In other words, your thoughts create your life.

It is therefore not surprising that the successful people Hill interviewed had learned to cultivate their thoughts in a way that empowered them. Whether you see the worst-case scenario that can happen or the best-case scenario, in both instances the situation has only occurred in your mind. Yet, the scenario you envision will eventually manifest itself and become your reality.

IT SEEMS so simple, and yet so many people operate on the basis of their fears. In our modern day, six (additional) universal fears have been identified that hold people back.

—⁓—

What are you afraid of? Here are some of the things you may fear.

The Unknown. How often do you go to the same restaurant and order the same thing on the menu? As humans we are creatures of habit, and although not everybody acts on it to the same extent, most of us are afraid of the unknown. We don't like the uncertainty that comes with the unknown. The key is not to let this fear stop you from exploring new possibilities. The only way you can grow and improve your life is to step outside your comfort zone and welcome the unknown.

Pain. Of course nobody likes to be in pain. It's not strange that we will do everything we can to avoid pain. Yet, when your thoughts of being in pain are so dominantly present that they prevent you from taking action, you need to change your focus. In many cases the pain caused by thinking about the possibility of pain is worse than actually experiencing it. Imagined pain can be just as harmful as real pain—sometimes even more harmful!

Loss. Whether you are afraid to lose somebody you love, your house, your job, or your business, in every case the fear of loss takes away from enjoying what you still have. In the past several years many have had to deal with financial challenges. It is understandable to be concerned when people around you get laid off, but it won't do you any good to be anxious about something that may or may not happen. As Napoleon Hill pointed out, your vibration of fear increases the chance of losing your job.

Judgment. We want people to like and appreciate us. We want to belong and be part of a community or group. That is why we are afraid to be judged. We don't want others to view us as crazy or wrong, because that would mean we don't fit in anymore. Sometimes fear of judgment means that our greatest ideas are buried without ever having the chance to grow into something incredible. Have the courage to be yourself. You can overcome the fear of judgment by viewing other people's comments as feedback, or just their opinion—nothing more. That way you won't have to feel judged.

Success. This fear seems somewhat odd. You may wonder, "Why would I be afraid of success?" Unfortunately it is more prevalent than you might think. Some people don't follow through on projects, or even sabotage relationships (often subconsciously), when they feel that the next level of success is more than they can handle. This fear is related to the fear of the unknown, and is also closely tied to self-doubt. If we don't think we are deserving of success, we are more likely to somehow prevent ourselves from achieving it. Rest assured, we are all deserving!

Failure. Every successful person can tell you that they have failed more times than anyone else. It all boils down to your perception of failure. When you see every time you fail as a learning opportunity and a stepping-stone, the fear of failure will have no power over you. *Fail forward fast.* Isn't that how we all learned to walk? You will come to realize that as long as you learn from the experience, making mistakes really isn't such a big deal. It is part of the road to success.

Fear is a misuse of the imagination.

Fear will stop progress in its tracks. Making decisions begets advancement. Once you can take control of these demons, you will find peace of mind and accelerate fast in the direction of your dreams. You don't have to allow fear to control your thoughts, and thus your reality. What if changing your life is as simple as making a decision?

"If you're in a place right now where you feel stuck or depressed, know that you are in control of your environment!" Sharon declared. "Don't let fear paralyze you. Take that fear and let it motivate you. Don't be alone, go out and collaborate. If you add value to another's life, you will add value to your life."

The first step is becoming aware of the fears that affect you most, because you can't change what you don't acknowledge.

Take the time to analyze your life, your decisions, your actions, and your results. Be honest with yourself. Have any of the fears mentioned above held you back?

Decide to overcome your fear. Yes, you have the power to transform your anxiety into love, desire, enthusiasm, freedom, and hope.

HOW CAN YOU OVERCOME THE "GHOSTS OF FEAR"?

Vibrations of Success

You can do tremendous things and attain all you want in life, as Hill's research proves. Don't allow fear to halt your expansion and development. Let your vibrations of success be stronger than those of fear.

Create Your Own Reality

Don't allow other people's opinions or commercial propaganda to fill your mind with doubt and fear, because this will create your reality. Base your thoughts on courage and faith and your mind will make that your reality. Decide to be in control of your own thoughts.

Direct Your Thoughts

Remember that fear is a state of mind. You will attract what you focus on, so consciously direct your thoughts to your definite major purpose and to living a fulfilling life. See yourself as financially secure instead of losing yourself in the stack of bills.

CHAPTER 7

More Than a Wish

IT IS A MOVIE WITH A LOT OF EMOTIONAL TWISTS AND turns—and it focuses on one moral choice that threatens to end a young couple's marriage almost before it has begun. You may remember seeing it: *Indecent Proposal.* It's not one of the greatest films of all time, but there are some interesting lessons embedded in the story of a beautiful young woman's choice about whether to spend the night with a super-wealthy man, who looks suspiciously like Robert Redford, for a million dollars . . . and then there's her husband, who must agree to the bargain—all three are grown-ups and have free will. The economic consequences of the husband's consent are almost unimaginable, but it's the personal cost that he and his wife will pay that is the killer.

Woody Harrelson plays the husband, and Demi Moore is the wife. Harrelson is a teacher and is nowhere near wealthy. Moore wants the best for her husband, whom she loves, and the best for them as a couple. A tough choice to make . . . or is it?

Meanwhile, in his classroom, Woody Harrelson delivers the best line in the whole movie. He holds up a brick and asks his students, "What is this?" Now, there's a single, simple, correct answer to his question: it's a brick. Everyone gets that one right.

Except they did not immediately understand the intent of the question. The teacher tells the kids the *true* answer, something they wouldn't naturally think of at all. He says: "Even a brick wants to be something."

And why not? It's believable. A brick by itself is nothing, really. But a brick used to build the Taj Mahal or the Notre Dame Cathedral in Paris is really something—a part of a great edifice—something big and beautiful.

After all, who wouldn't want to be a part of something like that? Even a brick. Even bricks have dreams . . .

One of the pillars—in fact the very first step toward riches—in Napoleon Hill's philosophy, as expounded in *Think and Grow Rich*, is desire. It is the starting point of all achievement: a definite desire. It holds great power, the power contained in a seed that can grow into an immense and sturdy tree.

Hill gets down to cases and illustrates just what he means about a burning desire as absolutely essential to success. He uses the case of a simple and definite desire for *riches* to lay out his method in six practical steps.

FIRST. Fix in your mind the exact amount of money you desire. Be definite as to the amount.

SECOND. Determine exactly what you intend to give in return for the money you desire. (There is no such thing as "something for nothing.")

THIRD. Establish a definite date when you intend to possess the money you desire.

FOURTH. Create a definite plan for carrying out your desire, and begin at once, whether you are ready or not, to put this plan into action.

FIFTH. Write out a clear, concise statement of the amount of money you intend to acquire, name the time limit for its acquisition, state what you intend to give in return for the money, and describe clearly the plan through which you intend to accumulate it.

SIXTH. Read your written statement aloud, twice daily, once just before retiring at night, and once after rising in the morning. As you read, see and feel and believe yourself already in possession of the money.

In this regard, it helps not to be a brick. But you have to have at least as much desire as the average brick. And you ought to develop your sense of timing so you can seize the opportune moment—the defining moment. The moment to be something, to achieve your goal, whether it's the acquisition of money or the launch of a new business venture. You've got to want it, to have within you the burning desire Hill describes so well. And always remember:

Even a brick wants to be something.

———

Make a Wish

"Mommy," Chris said, "when I grow up I want to be a police officer." His mother, Linda, smiled at her son's pronouncement. As long he was willing to fight, she would not give up hoping for a miracle. It broke her heart to see her little boy suffer. The odds were against him, as the doctors had given Chris only a few more weeks to live.

Like many boys his age, his heroes were Ponch and Jon from the popular old TV show *CHiPs*, which featured the adventures of two California Highway Patrol officers. Watching *CHiPs* was one of the few things that brought joy to his world and kept Chris going. Leukemia had ravaged his body and he was fighting for his life.

As Frank Shankwitz cruised down the Beeline Highway on his motorcycle, miles from civilization, patches of wildflowers danced in the crisp breeze. He felt there was something special about the day. The hiss of his radio startled him, as the dispatcher's voice rang loud in his ear.

"Can you copy a 21 [telephone] number?" she asked.

"Stand by," Frank said as he pulled to the side of the empty road.

"Can you check out a 21 and call Detective Ron Cox?" Frank drove to the nearest pay phone and called Ron, a fellow officer and longtime friend.

Little did he know how deeply this phone call would affect his life—and the hundreds of thousands of lives he would touch thereafter.

On the call, Ron told Frank about a little boy named Chris Greicius who dreamed of becoming a police officer. Frank was sad to learn that the boy was dying and didn't have much time left. Chris was on his way to the department in a helicopter and

Ron asked if Frank wanted to meet him there and show him his bike.

"Of course," Frank said. He was more than happy to bring a little sunshine to the poor kid.

When the helicopter landed, Frank and a few others were waiting in uniform to greet him. Naturally, Frank and the others expected paramedics to wheel out a very ill boy in a wheelchair. Instead, Chris leaped out of the helicopter, full of excitement.

The bond between Chris and Frank was immediate.

Chris's mother was thrilled. She looked on as Frank rode Chris around on his bike. In that moment her little boy was a normal seven-year-old—all traces of sickness temporarily masked by the elated expression on his face.

Frank was moved. He had never before been somebody's hero.

As far as Chris was concerned, he might as well have stepped right onto the set of *CHiPs*. The youngster was taken on a tour of the armory and the compound, given his own "Arizona Highway Patrol" badge, and made the first and only Honorary Patrolman in the history of the Arizona Highway Patrol.

Chris was doing so well that at the end of the day, the doctor told his mother that he could be home with her instead of going back to the hospital.

Returning home that night, Frank was deeply touched by his new friend, and wanted to do something that would keep the memory alive for him. As inspiration struck, Frank found a tailor to get a police uniform custom made for the boy.

The next morning Frank picked up the fitted garment from the tailor, who had worked on it all night to have it ready in time. Walking up to Chris's front door with officers at his side, Frank couldn't help but smile. He rang the doorbell and Linda Bergendahl-Pauling, Chris's mother, was happily surprised to see him.

"Come on in, officer," she said.

Within a few minutes, Chris came running down the stairs.

"Hey, Chris," Frank said, as he gave the boy a hug, "I brought you something very special." He handed the box to the boy and added, "This is your uniform. Now you are a motor-cycle officer!"

Chris's eyes lit up and his excitement was evident as he bounced off the walls, again hiding any signs of illness. He quickly threw his new garb on and proudly paraded through the house. Suddenly he noticed something was missing.

"Officer Frank, my uniform doesn't have wings like yours does. How can I earn my wings?"

Frank and the other officers jokingly said, "If we had a course, we could have you take it."

It didn't take Chris long to come up with a solution.

In no time, the young lad came back with a small battery-operated motorcycle his mother had given him in place of a wheelchair.

Soon, the officers were setting up cones for him to ride through. They devised some simple maneuvers for Chris to navigate as if it were a real test. After several accomplished exercises, Chris held his head up high.

"You passed, Chris," the officers told him.

"So when will I get my wings?" Chris asked impatiently.

"You have officially earned your wings, Chris," Frank replied. "I promise I'll get them for you."

The pride was beaming from the boy's spirit and it brought a soft tear to his mother's eye.

Instead of heading home after their time together, Frank went straight to the uniform shop to order the wings, which needed to be hand-crafted especially for Chris.

Despite his exciting day, Chris's condition worsened that evening, and he was rushed to the hospital. When Frank arrived with the wings, he was notified that Chris was in a deep coma and the doctors feared that he would not come out. His mother was naturally devastated—yet the uniform hanging next to his bed softened her pain, as she recalled the wonderful time he had been able to enjoy.

"At least he has realized his dream of becoming a police officer," she said to Frank when he walked into the room and placed his arm around her in comfort.

"We have to make him an official officer, with wings this time," Frank said, as he pinned the symbol on Chris's uniform.

Like a scene in a movie, it was at this very moment that Chris's eyes opened. He asked, "Officer Frank, does that mean that I am an official motorcycle officer?"

When the young man's hero said that he was, the seven-year-old boy sat up straight, smiling, laughing, and talking to his mom in a tone that made it seem like Christmas morning. The excitement was overwhelming, in the best sense of the word. Crying in happiness, Linda knew this was the best moment her son had ever experienced.

Later that day, Chris passed away peacefully, but not without leaving behind a legacy that would change the lives of hundreds of thousands of children all over the world.

After a full police-honored funeral, Chris was buried in his uniform—with wings and all. His grave marker reads, "Chris Greicius, Arizona Trooper."

Frank Shankwitz had been deeply moved by this whole experience.

For a brief time, Chris had forgotten he was sick. He was just a little boy again, having fun. His mother was so happy, too. It caused Frank to ask why they couldn't do that for other children. Why not let children like Chris make a wish that others could help to grant?

When Frank returned from Chris's funeral, he contacted a friend who was an attorney and another friend who was an accountant. Almost in no time, they helped him set up a 501(c)(3), and within six months, in November 1980, the Make-A-Wish Foundation was official.

Thanks to the massive media response, many people started to contribute to the organization. Frank was interviewed by newspapers and radio and television stations, locally and nationwide. Although he didn't have a lot of money, Frank gave what he had—his love, dedication, and time.

Even when he experienced financially challenging times of his own, Frank Shankwitz and his better half *never* took a penny from the foundation. All the money was used to make wishes come true.

He and his wife embodied the *stickability* message. No matter how tough things got, they never gave up on the dream, never gave in to the challenges along the journey.

Four years before meeting Chris, Frank had been in a serious motorcycle accident. He had actually died at the scene, but was resuscitated minutes later by a nurse who happened to be nearby.

Although he made a full recovery, the experience left him wondering, "Why me? Why was I given another chance to live?"

Now, he had found his answer: his purpose was to start the Make-A-Wish Foundation. It began from his kitchen table, and he often worked at the police station whenever he could find the time in between his regular daily tasks. Fortunately, his commander was very supportive and allowed him to do whatever he had to for the fledgling foundation as long as he worked his usual eight hours a day for the station.

Frank's journey was not without challenges though. Finding the time and the resources was a continuous struggle. It required considerable ingenuity and *stickability* to grant the variety of wishes of the children.

Once the foundation was a living entity, it was time to grant its first official wish. The first official Make-A-Wish child was a Hispanic boy named Bopsy, who simply wanted to go to Disneyland. Every time Frank called the theme park to discuss his charity, they would hang up on him.

Finally one day Frank decided he had to come up with a new strategy.

This time, he called and asked to speak with the director. He said, "My name is Frank Shankwitz and I am with the Arizona Patrol. One of your people has come through Arizona and got a ticket. There is a warrant out for his arrest. We need to get together and take care of this."

Once he had the director's attention, Frank confessed, "Okay, I lied. You can call my boss and have me fired, but here's what I need, and it's for a good reason."

A week later, Bopsy was on a plane to Disneyland, and Disney became one of the Make-A-Wish Foundation's biggest sponsors.

There's always another way.

Although some people didn't believe Frank could do it, and he would feel overwhelmed, exhausted, and on the verge of giving up, it was usually at that moment somebody would tell him about another child about to receive a wish. This always inspired him to get back on his feet and say, "We can't quit. We've got to do this for the kids."

Shankwitz realized that when you put others first, the rewards are immeasurable. Where would you be if you could do something bigger than yourself? Sometimes the greatest accomplishments come from the smallest of intentions.

Frank didn't set out to change the world—he simply wanted to help one boy. Thank goodness he did. Frank's greatest fulfillment now comes from knowing the difference he's made in the lives of so many children who are fighting life-threatening diseases.

Having a wish granted has a profound effect on the healing process. Statistics show that 70 percent of the Make-A-Wish children win the battle with their disease and actually survive.

For Frank, the biggest thrill is when he steps off the stage after giving a presentation and an adult comes up to him and says, "I want to introduce myself, I'm a wish child!" Frank looks into their eyes and asks, "What was your wish?"

As they share their journey, Franks says you can literally see them reliving the wish as if they were experiencing it for the first time.

Throughout history there have been remarkable people just like Frank Shankwitz, who devoted themselves to a cause greater than themselves—with phenomenal results.

Mother Teresa, the Catholic nun from Albania, saw the suffering and poverty of the people outside the walls of her convent in Calcutta, India, and it made a deep impression on her. So deep, in fact, that it inspired her to leave a life that, though by no means luxurious, at least provided everything she needed to live comfortably. Instead she lived on the streets with the oppressed and disadvantaged in the worst parts of the city. As a devoutly religious woman, she no doubt recalled the core teaching of Christianity: there is more happiness in giving than there is in receiving. Her gift to those in desperate need—the poorest of the poor and the sickest of the sick—became legendary.

Mohandas Gandhi spent twenty-one years in South Africa, where he witnessed firsthand the brutal oppressions and injustices of apartheid. On one occasion he was thrown off a train for refusing to leave the first-class compartment, simply because of his skin color. On another, he was beaten for not making room for a European passenger. He was also barred from hotels and persecuted for wearing a turban. These events awoke in him a desire to rectify injustices, as well as making him question what European rule meant for his own people. Surely he wasn't the only one to suffer at the hands of Europeans for nothing more than not being white. The rest of his life was a testament to the lessons he learned as a victim of oppression, and the decision he made to do something about it. In fact, he led India to freedom as a modern state.

Regardless of your opinion of these two memorable figures, there's no doubt that they left an impression on our world. Their *stickability* and utter devotion to their causes are sources of inspiration for us all.

THREE THINGS WE CAN LEARN FROM THIS:

Have a cause that is greater than you.

BY FOCUSING on others rather than on yourself, you'll be motivated to push past obstacles others find insurmountable.

Surround yourself with people who believe in you and your cause.

IN ORDER to succeed, you need people around you who can help you. Say good-bye to the negative people who want to talk you out of it and find people who share your passion and commitment.

Give back to others.

YOU MAY not be the next Mother Teresa, Mohandas Gandhi, or Frank Shankwitz, and that is okay. Even when you don't have the desire or resources to set up your own foundation, there is always something you can do for somebody else. How can you contribute to making the world a better place? What simple step can you take today on the path to selfless giving to others?

CHAPTER 8

The Belief of
One Person

—◦◦◦—

"GENE, YOU CAN'T DO THAT!" FRANK LOOKED AT HIM AS if he had lost his mind. "You and I have been good friends for a long time and I have to be honest with you. I mean, do you have any idea how much money and energy we spend to kill all the rats in our hotels? Now you are telling me that you are going to have a rat deliver food? It's crazy!"

As the CEO of Holiday Inn, Frank knew a thing or two about business, and Gene Landrum had always respected his opinion.

On this day, however, it didn't take long for Gene to realize that this conversation closely resembled countless others he had experienced over the years. Every other expert he had met along the road simply could not see what Gene saw.

And now it was Frank's turn to voice his unshakable proclivity for traditionalism—he was unable to progress beyond *the way things have always been.*

Gene's situation reminded him of Walt Disney, the creative genius who was willing to use his own money to create Mickey Mouse, Pinocchio, and the many other Disney characters that have become cultural icons for well over half a century.

Just because it hadn't been done before, didn't make it a bad idea.

When Disney shared his idea with others, even his own brother said, "It's the stupidest thing I've ever heard." People told him it could not be done, but he never gave up, he never stopped, and he refused to listen to all the people who told him "no."

Like Walt Disney, many visionaries have had to tune out the "experts" from time to time—not to mention their own family. As Gary W. Goldstein put it (remember him from Chapter 4?), sometimes it's best to *pass on the pass!*

Obviously, at this encounter, Frank could not see the vision Gene was sharing. "How could he not see it?" Gene thought. His new and innovative restaurant would be the perfect family entertainment.

The idea struck him one day when he started thinking about where a family could go on a Friday night with their children. He theorized that Grandpa and Grandma probably don't want to go to a fast food restaurant any more than their four-year-old granddaughter would choose a fancy restaurant. Gene saw an opportunity for compromise.

Families would love a place where kids could have fun and adults could enjoy good food at the same time. What he envisioned turned out to be brilliant! Still, though, he had to face the fact that no one else shared his enthusiasm. *No one.*

Little did he know that on one historic day, all that was about to change.

Returning to his day job at Atari, where he is credited with writing the specs for the original Atari 600 game programming system, Gene Landrum was greeted by Atari founder Nolan Bushnell.

"Good to see you, Nolan," Gene said, as he stepped into the board room with a tall latte in his hand.

The directors of Atari sat in a conference room boasting floor-to-ceiling windows. The natural light flooded into the spacious environment where creative ideas flourished and innovative thinkers were welcomed with open arms. In their previous meeting, they had brainstormed to find a way to get computer games into more friendly gathering places, or even restaurants. (Since the first pinball machines were invented in the 1930s, arcade games had been widely associated with negative things such as gangs and drugs. These types of games were largely found in seedy bars in rough areas of town.)

"How is your business plan coming along, Gene?" Nolan asked excitedly, referring to the Wild Rat Idea, which Gene had shared with him, too.

Gene took a sip of his morning brew and responded, "Well, I finished writing the business plan, drew up the floor plan, and even created the menu. All the details are in here." When Gene had broached the idea at their last meeting, most of the board members were skeptical. While he had his own reservations, Nolan wanted to see what Gene could do with his "crazy" idea.

Now Gene Landrum was ready to share a detailed outline and overview of the business plan with the board of directors. After his presentation, Nolan exclaimed, "Wow! That is pretty cool, man! I'll tell you what I'll do; I'll give you a million bucks—you go and build one."

"Really?" Gene was shocked, "You're giving me a million dollars? I am a high-tech marketing guy. I wouldn't even give myself a million dollars. I can't even spell restaurant, let alone build one!"

Nolan laughed, "I believe in you, Gene. Go make it happen!"

Thus, a star was born.

Just as Disney had done with a skinny mouse, Gene was

about to do with a rat. He figured that gang members wouldn't want to hang out at a place where a funny rat character was delivering pizza. He was right!

In 1977, Gene Landrum built the very first Chuck E. Cheese's restaurant in San Jose, California. He went on to build ninety-nine more. Without Nolan's support, the dream might never have come to fruition.

We need others to champion our ideas, as crazy as they might seem initially. It takes just one other person to push you over the hump toward greatness. It takes just one person to believe in you, perhaps even more than you believe in yourself.

Gene learned from this experience that big ideas live right on the edge—the wilder the idea, the more on the edge.

As Gene says, "Sure, you will fail a bunch, but when you finally win, you win really big. Those who don't risk much can't lose much, and conversely they will also have very little reward."

Touring the nation these days, Gene Landrum gives inspirational talks and shares a message that we shouldn't play to be safe. He emphasizes that if you are on the same track as everybody else, you won't end up getting anywhere. Take the road less traveled. Visionaries are willing to go where the pack won't.

As happened to many people in this book, (so called) expert after expert told Gene that his idea was stupid, including the owner of the biggest pizza place in town. (Note: eighteen months later, Chuck E. Cheese's sales had surpassed his.)

Gene was recently inducted into the CEO Hall of Fame. In his acceptance speech, he shared a simple story that explained how he rose to the top in spite of what the masses predicted.

Vision is seeing something coming long before everybody else sees it going.

"You have to see the big picture. It is critical to the process. Understand that 88 percent of the world is left-brain dominant and will never see the essence of what you are doing. Once you do get your vision on track, the key element for long-term success comes from creating an experience."

Gene continued: "One day a father wanted to treat his daughter to a special day out and he took her to Chuck E. Cheese's. When I asked him how he liked it, he said, 'I love it, I love it. My daughter loves it. Look, she is over there playing games. We love your pizza. There is just one thing: I heard you had that rat. I would like him to come out, so I can take a picture with him and my daughter. He hasn't been out and we have been here for an hour.' I went to the back, found the manager, and said, 'The policy is that the rat comes out every twenty minutes. What is the problem?' The manager, irritated, answered, 'Two kids didn't show up tonight. Do you want the pizza out or that stupid rat?' Clearly the manager didn't see the big picture. That father drove from Menlo Park to San Jose to take his daughter to Chuck E. Cheese's. On the way he had probably passed about eighty-seven pizza joints. He didn't come for the pizza—he came for his daughter to be entertained."

Many business owners make the same mistake and don't know the business they are truly in. Chuck E. Cheese's is not in the pizza business, but in the family-entertainment business.

That rat made an appearance and, yes, the father and daughter finally got their photo taken. All because someone finally believed in Gene's idea—just one person, and sometimes that's all it takes.

We need others to believe in us and support us. But the first person who must believe in you . . . is you!

Belief is more than possible—it is as necessary as breathing.

Which leads us to Nik Halik's story . . .

Every weekday at 3:30 p.m. the neighborhood kids would walk by Nik's window laughing and talking on their way home from school. He desperately wanted to be just like them, but his asthma (or more precisely, the medication doctors had prescribed for his asthma), made him so sick that he could not go to school with the other kids. Each day, he knew the boys would be outside playing soccer after they had changed out of their school clothes. He didn't want to be stuck in his room any longer, so one day he grabbed his ball and ran into the kitchen.

"Mommy, can I please go and play with my friends?" young Nik asked, with his soccer ball under his arm. "Please, Mommy!" His begging eyes did not persuade his mother.

"I'm sorry," his mother replied. "You are too sick to go outside. You have to stay in bed."

"Please!" The little boy tried one more time.

"No, son, I would like you to go back to your bed," his mother answered in an unyielding tone.

Nik realized that his begging was in vain and returned to his room, but not without grabbing another volume of the *Encyclopaedia Britannica* from the bookshelf.

A few weeks before, a traveling salesman had come to the house and performed his song and dance, trying to convince Nik's parents that the thick volumes of the encyclopedia would help their children with their homework and offer an opportunity to advance their learning.

Nik's parents were immigrants to Australia, each from a poor Greek family, and didn't speak much English. They were dedicated to improving the future of their four children and willing to make the financial investment. They were committed to giving their children the best education—no matter the sacrifices.

His siblings gathered excitedly behind their parents as they spoke with the salesman. Nik jumped up and down in excitement, yelling, "Let's get them! Let's get them!"

Little did he know at that time how much this skilled salesman would impact the course of his life.

Holding the heavy volume with both hands, the eager young boy went back to his room. He kicked off his sneakers and jumped onto his bed. The *Encyclopaedia Britannica* allowed him to travel beyond the confinement of his room. It opened his eyes and his imagination to a completely new world. He had read about faraway countries, exotic places, the pyramids in Egypt, the impressive galaxies that make up our universe, and much more. All of these discoveries were breathtaking to the eight-year-old boy.

Nik grabbed a pen and paper. In that moment, even without consciously knowing it, he changed his destiny. He started to dream and imagine what it would be like to actually visit the countries he was reading about, so he could experience the smell, taste the exotic fruits, and meet these fascinating people from different cultures. He could see himself on the top of the highest mountain in the world.

"That would be so cool!" he thought to himself. "I can be just like Tintin, going on magical adventures."

He was a mountain climber, a pilot, a space explorer. He dived down to the deepest abyss of the ocean to explore shipwrecks. Once he started to think about the infinite possibilities and adventures life had to offer, he grew more and more excited.

With a stroke of a pen, he solidified his dreams on paper. The eight-year-old had a big vision for his life when he designed his Top 10 List (what nowadays we call a "bucket list"—the things he wanted to accomplish before he died).

Walk on the moon

Go to the space station on a rocket and live there

Become an astronaut

Own beautiful places all over the world

Travel and explore more than one hundred countries

Go to the bottom of the ocean and have lunch at the *Titanic*

Become a mountain climber and climb the highest mountain in the world

Run with the bulls in Spain

Become a millionaire

Become a rock-and-roll star

Nik never let go of his dreams. By writing them down, he effectively turned his dreams into *goals*. Sometimes he'd stay awake past midnight, dreaming about the things he was going to pursue in life, and imagining the world that was out there waiting for him.

Most children have had a dream or some wild idea, but often they forget about it, or they let others steal their dream. Not Nik.

His father, a hardworking truck driver, did not want his son to be disappointed, and told him, "You have asthma, you are nearsighted, and you are failing mathematics. These are three reasons why you will never ever become an astronaut. Stop wasting your time dreaming about it."

Of course, young Nik felt shattered, yet despite his father's words he stayed focused on the adventurous life he wanted to live.

How did he overcome his dad's discouragement? He didn't allow his father's limiting belief of what was possible to hold him back. Once he got outside the walls of his bedroom, he didn't want to be like anyone else.

In thirty-four years Nik has achieved eight out of the ten goals on his bucket list, and the remaining two are about to be achieved.

At age fourteen he started his first business. When he was eighteen, he had saved enough money to go to Los Angeles and realize his dream of becoming a rock star. Although his father still did not share his vision, his mother supported him in his goals and Nik remained unstoppable.

He became a millionaire at age twenty-four, but for Nik, life has always been about the magic, not about materialism. Smart wealth-building allowed him to become a multimillionaire and use his money to fund his other dreams, one of them of becoming an astronaut. (He paid $3 million for the training and $27 million for the flight.)

Nik had many outrageous experiences that far exceeded even his own ambitious bucket list—sleeping in an old jail in French Guyana and spending the night in a pyramid in Egypt are just a couple.

How did Nik make his dreams a reality? And how can you?

Decide what you want and write it down.

CHOOSE your thoughts to construct your picture of prosperity, in order for it to be manifested. Nik cultivated his mind, allowing it to blossom beyond his expectations. The quality of your thinking determines the quality of your life.

Stay focused.

NIK REALIZED that he needed money, a lot of money, to make his dreams come true. He was focused on generating wealth. For instance, he didn't own a car or a yacht, because both would depreciate.

Know your way.

THERE MAY be lonely times, and knowing your way will help you to stay on track. One time, Nik was stuck alone in an ice storm on Christmas Day. When all his friends and family were enjoying a lavish Christmas dinner, he was melting ice to make some tea.

Be accountable to yourself.

MOST PEOPLE give up way too quickly. What do you represent on this planet? It's the legacy you leave behind, the footprints you leave in history that count. What will be your gift to the world?

Travel, travel, travel.

YOU'LL CONTINUE to grow as a person. Never underestimate the value of personal development.

Enjoy the greatness of the moment!

REMEMBER that life in the real world rarely goes according to plan.

Nik and Gene are inspirational examples of what is possible when we stay true to our dreams. Enlist the support of just one other person and *believe in yourself, always*. That is the *stickability* factor! No matter what other people tell you, stay focused. Focus on the passions and motivations that radiate an abundance of vitality and energy in your life, rather than just the size of your wallet. Live a true life instead of simply existing.

Make your life an epic, extraordinary adventure.

CHAPTER 9

Defining Moments

—◦◦◦—

AN IMMIGRANT TO AMERICA FROM WHAT IS NOW CROA-
tia at the turn of the nineteenth century exemplified a new way
of thinking about science that helped set the stage for the revolution in technology that has impacted billions of lives across
the globe.

Nikola Tesla wanted to work for Thomas Edison, the reign-
ing genius of science and invention in the late 1900s. So, in
1884, the twenty-eight-year-old Tesla shipped out from France
and arrived in New York Harbor with a few cents in his pocket
and a letter of recommendation from a former employer, who
wrote, "I know two great men and you are one of them; the
other is this young man."

The two geniuses did not hit it off very well. Edison angered Tesla by reneging on the promise of a reward after the younger man succeeded with a major project that others had failed to accomplish, and Tesla left Edison's employment. He formed his own company and began to patent his numerous inventions and earn fees and royalties for his work in the field of electricity.

Tesla was a unique character with a unique vision in a unique moment in history. He went his own way and developed his own theories about the physical universe, sometimes in conflict with those of the greatest minds of the time, including Edison and Einstein. But he was one of the most unselfish geniuses ever, and he worked not to accumulate personal wealth but to enrich the lives of all human beings. And he succeeded to a great degree.

Napoleon Hill would call Tesla's great gift "specialized knowledge"—that is, something that sets a person apart from all others and helps to define his worth and can be the basis for his wealth. The key to specialized knowledge, however, is not merely having it, but *sharing* it. That's what Nikola Tesla did throughout his life. Even as a very private person (he never married) who habitually worked long hours in isolation and did not socialize a great deal, he held humanity in his heart and strongly believed that energy should be *free* the world over.

In this, as in all aspects of his life and personality, Tesla held nothing back. He was what he was, and he frankly couldn't have cared less what others thought of him, as long as he could communicate his ideas.

Transparency is when you stop hiding the uncomfortable parts of yourself.

Naturally, the thought of offering free energy did not sit well with the business moguls of the day.

Tesla theorized that the earth itself was the greatest conductor of energy and the source of all life (in a spiritual as well as a scientific sense, though Tesla did not believe in any particular religion). Therefore, the brilliant physicist and engineer, inventor of the Tesla coil and countless other breakthroughs in the science of energy, staked out a lonely position, but one he thought was right—for scientific and humanitarian reasons.

Tesla was willing to be shunned by his fellow scientists and those who believed only in the singular pursuit of profit over all other goals. He had nothing against business, but the development of knowledge for its own sake, and for the benefit of mankind, was his primary focus. He could not conceive of *not* sharing such knowledge with the widest possible audience.

And throughout his life, until the end, when he died alone and virtually penniless—by choice—he stuck to that principle, no matter the cost. Indeed, like many of the people in this book, he paid dearly for his nearly obsessive focus on the achievement of goals that were beyond the reach of most men. The defining moment for Nikola Tesla came early in his relationship with Thomas Edison. Having made the decision to chart his own course and seek the truth beneath the science he loved, he never looked back.

Nikola Tesla recognized the opportunity in his time—ahead of his time, really—for collaboration on a global basis to solve critical problems, particularly in the field of energy, and for people to come together across borders and biases to serve one another. Are we ready to listen to the clear voice of such a prophet today? Do we recognize *our* defining moment when it lies right in front of us, and would we be willing to offer this opportunity to the world free of charge?

⁓

Matt Mullenweg was a nineteen-year-old college student living in Houston. He studied political science and loved to play jazz saxophone. By all appearances he was a nice, normal kid going to school—growing up and having fun.

But there was far more to Matt than college parties and impromptu jam sessions. Not only did he know how to write computer software code, but he could do it extraordinarily well.

He got involved with open source communities. These were communities based not on who you knew, or what your last name was, or what kind of car you drove, but based purely on *merit*. The open source communities were meritocracies in the traditional sense, and cared only about what Matt was doing. What he was doing was writing code at a very high level and contributing to the common open source effort.

Generally, "open source" refers to a philosophy that promotes free distribution and access to an end product's design and implementation details. This means a program's source code is available to the general public for use or modification from its original design, free of charge. We refer to open source *communities* because these source codes are typically created as a collaborative effort in which programmers like Matt improve upon the code and share the changes with the community. These communities came about as a response to proprietary software owned by corporations.

Matt quickly developed a stellar reputation as a software programmer. What he loved most was the fact that only his performance mattered—that is, only what he contributed to the growing open source movement. He felt like he was a part of something larger than himself, doing his part to refine it and make it better. This was an incredibly liberating concept for him. It created a true equality of opportunity within a baseline of resources and access.

The moment came when Matt realized what he needed to do. Against the advice of many close to him, he left the University of Houston before graduating to take a job at CNET Networks. In late 2005, he quit his job at CNET and founded Automattic. One thing led to another, and soon the result of Matt Mullenweg's efforts was WordPress, a free and open source blogging tool and content management system.

As of December 2011, WordPress version 3.0 had been downloaded more than 65 million times. It is currently the most popular blogging system in use on the Internet and powers more than 50 million blogs globally, and 14.7 percent of the top million Web sites in the world.

Twenty-two out of every hundred new active domains in the United States run this program. In April 2012 the Web site monitoring service Pingdom reported that "WordPress completely dominates the top 100 blogs" and is used by 49 percent of the top one hundred blogs in the world.

In May 2012, the technology Web site All Things D reported that "Wordpress now powers 70 million sites and expects to bring in $45 million in revenue this year." The company's success is also reflected in its incredibly low rate of staff attrition—WordPress currently has 106 employees and has only ever hired 118.

Matt has accomplished extraordinary things for someone who has yet to celebrate his thirtieth birthday. Despite his youth, Matt's personal philosophy and sage advice transcends generations and reflects the universal principles of success.

Matt believes that the key to the whole software development process is getting the right people around the table, aligning their goals, and creating the mind-set of listening, watching, and of course *using* the software. From experience Matt knows that a lot of people who build software don't use it themselves. His philosophy is that it is very important for designers to use their own product.

While Matt isn't much for conventional corporate structure, he knows that certain precepts, like trust, are vital to any productive working relationship. It is also vital, he believes, to be able to learn quickly and determine which opportunities to seize.

In software programming, or any field, our success is largely based on our ability and willingness to spot the right opportunities. If we keep our eyes and hearts open, those opportunities are constant and they are everywhere. This is what are called our *defining moments*. Often these are not served on a silver platter. Often nobody tells us when or where these op-portunities occur. Like Matt, we must develop the ability to clearly see when a moment comes along that can help us define who we are.

Being able to find the right opportunity within infinite pos-sibilities is only the beginning. We must be able to *seize* and *stick*.

What does *stickability* mean to Matt Mullenweg?

"I would say that it's a primary quality we look for when hiring people, because it doesn't matter exactly what skills you have, or what you know today, or what it is that you do, *it's your ability to learn and persevere in the future that really determines your success*. I think you need to have a love of learning and a sort of an innate curiosity and also that stick-to-it-iveness.

"In technology, we're afforded the incredible opportunity of being able to ship a new product every day of the week, every hour of the day. In that context we typically plan two to three months out, but along the way we are constantly adjust-ing course based on data, based on usage, based on feedback, based on how we like it, based on everything else going on in the world. When it comes to *stickability*, it's about exercising your mental muscle.

"I've certainly made mistakes along the way, but if you keep in mind the core principles of what's really important to you, hopefully the external circumstances afforded by your success will not determine where you spend the bulk of your time and your energy."

Matt's primary business goal is straightforward and yet incredibly difficult to accomplish: the democratization of publishing. He wants to empower writers and give them the tools to express themselves.

"I think that there is a very natural tension between visitors and authors," Matt explains. "As an author, what you want to do to is be distinct and stand out from the rest of the Web. So you add these widgets, doodads, and customizations, which end up often creating a cluttered experience. As a reader you would love to just see the text, no graphics, nothing except the information that you need to get your job done.

"With mobile, because most people don't pay attention to the bells and whistles, we created a uniform experience across all of our blogs that's very clean and fast. But as more people started to notice our movement toward simplicity, we got a ton of requests, good ones, asking us to let them change this and that. They wanted to have some of the same control over the mobile site that people do over their desktop versions of the site, which is ultimately why people love WordPress—because it provides that control."

What advice does Matt offer to Web site authors?

"The best writing advice I've heard, and occasionally practice, is to write every single day first thing in the morning. You wake up, put the coffee on the pot—do whatever you need to do—and just write a thousand words or two thousand words or something, just get it out there. And maybe you don't publish it, maybe you edit it down to a couple hundred, maybe it doesn't matter. But you're exercising that mental muscle. You're sort of tapping into some of the creativity you had when you were asleep. Free-flowing associations are also a good start to the day."

Matt's business philosophy is simple: he figures it out as he goes!

"Basically we know nothing; we just get on with it. We should embrace knowing nothing and keep an open mind, but avoid giving too much advice because I don't know the answer. I'm still figuring it out."

WordPress was conceived at a time when a keyboard and a mouse were the requisite tools for any type of user. Now, tablets and smartphones have completely changed how people interact and produce content, partly because they're so integrated. Matt considers this to be a defining moment for the industry.

"I do know that I would probably enjoy a lot less working in the world of, say, physical goods, where there's a year or two development process to ship one thing and you kind of get one at-bat," says Matt, applying an apt baseball analogy. "Our world is more like batting practice. There's a ball coming every thirty seconds, you can just take swings at it.

"We found, for example, that there was a piece of code on some new things we were working on that was taking about five hundred milliseconds to run, so it was delaying the page about half a second, which is pretty noticeable. One person started working on optimizing that function and got it down some, call it sixteen milliseconds. Then someone else said, 'What if we just remove it? What if we just don't do this thing at all?' If we remove the piece of code entirely we're down to, obviously, zero milliseconds. That ended up being the right answer."

Are the software visionaries of today fundamentally different from yesterday's pioneers? While Thomas Edison eventually created lightbulbs and phonographs, what he was really doing was experimenting—learning from thousands of failures before he created one success. Writing software code requires the exact same type of creative discipline and perseverance Edison employed in his lab.

"If we break it down, all these people we think of as creative geniuses have very similar habits," Matt believes. "They wake up in the morning and do whatever it is they do, over and over and over and over and over again! The public only sees their 'flashes of brilliance' that happen every so often. Sometimes these 'flashes' occur years or even decades apart.

"I feel like having anchors along the way allows you to take better risks. They allow you to be motivated for the right things, which in the software world is the user experience. It's a marathon, not a sprint. You don't want to be dealing with fire drills or payroll or things like that every two weeks, because it's going to be taking your mind off what really matters—what you're building."

Hear everything, *but filter what you listen to.*

Whether you're twenty-eight and living in San Francisco writing code, fifty-eight and sitting in a board room trying to manage a Fortune 500 company, or currently unemployed and looking for the right opportunity, the principles of *stickability* are the same.

HOW CAN WE IDENTIFY AND SEIZE A DEFINING MOMENT?

Contribute to something larger than yourself.

CONSIDER that the measure of true happiness is the extent to which we *give*. When we contribute to a cause greater than ourselves, we effectively find *purpose*. Remember that you are not alone. Finding purpose is a collaborative effort, as exemplified in Matt's case of contributing mightily to the open source movement.

Keep your ear to the ground.

OPPORTUNITIES are so amorphous and pervasive that it can sometimes be difficult to sort them all out—which one(s) shall we seize and when? Maintain an open mind at all times. Often, the best opportunities are the ones that initially seem the most risky. Never miss an opportunity to learn something and never miss an opportunity to be inspired—they are everywhere!

Be patient.

OFTENTIMES, the defining moments of our lives are only realized in hindsight. They cannot be forced nor forged. They might not be as distinct and grandiose as deciding to drop out of college to start a software company. This is okay. Remember that you are your own standard! Matt's story is inspirational not in the sense that we should all do what he did, but in the sense that we, too, can learn how to identify our own defining moments and have the *stickability* to seize them.

CHAPTER 10

Blind Faith

———

FOR THE VISIONARY NAPOLEON HILL, FAITH IS THE VI-
sualization of and belief in the attainment of desire. He counted
faith as the second step in his programmatic approach to the
attainment of wealth. In the chapter devoted to the subject, he
stated: "Faith is the head chemist of the mind. When faith is
blended with the vibration of thought, the subconscious mind
instantly picks up the vibration, translates it into its spiritual
equivalent, and transmits to Infinite Intelligence, as in the case
of prayer."

Hill advocated that one should have faith in oneself, as well
as faith in what he called the "Infinite." This is not a religious
statement, though men and women of various religions (or
none at all) can find support for their belief system in the phi-

losophy contained in *Think and Grow Rich*. Faith is, in fact, the starting point for all goals and the basis upon which all success is built.

The heights you can climb and the amount of wealth you can ultimately realize are limited primarily by you. Whether through fear—there are those Six Ghosts of Fear again!—or lack of faith (which can also be called lack of self-confidence), we are quite capable of stalling or sabotaging ourselves on any given day or in any given lifetime.

The decision lies with you. Hill saw this and gave us a blueprint for overcoming self-limitations. All we need apply is *stickability*! Anousheh Ansari and so many others we've met on this journey show us the power of faith in self despite all odds and obstacles.

But there is one story in particular that illustrates the point better than almost any other.

—◦◦◦—

It was just a routine physical. Jim thought nothing of it. Every high school football player must pass a medical exam in order to be eligible to play. All he had to do was go see the doctor, take a few tests, and get a clean bill of health. Then he could put on the pads and start to scrimmage.

With his rare combination of size and speed, Jim was being

recruited by top-tier colleges and would be a serious contender for the NFL someday. Playing ball was his only ambition. It was all he ever thought about. Football was his life.

But Jim didn't pass his exam.

Three different doctors told him he had an ocular disease. They said, "We're not sure why and we're not sure when, but someday you're going to be totally blind and there's nothing we can do about it."

Jim was devastated by the news. He made up his mind, however, that he was not going to let his vision problems ruin his athletic career. Although football was now no longer an option, he decided to focus on competitive weight lifting.

He devoted himself to the new sport with the same rigor of preparation and dedication he had for football. He was accustomed to intense workouts during the preseason for football, but nothing like this. Jim pushed himself to the next level in order to hone more specialized athletic skills. He spent countless hours in the weight room improving his technique, form, and strength. Meanwhile, he excelled in competition after competition and eventually rose to the level of national champion.

But he was not satisfied.

He wanted gold!

He began training for the U.S. Olympic team. After becoming national champion, Jim was poised and excited to lead the team into Moscow when forces out of his control interfered. The United States boycotted the 1980 Moscow Olympics in protest of the Soviet Union's invasion of Afghanistan.

For the other athletes this was a disappointment. They would have to continue training and compete four years later in the Los Angeles Olympics—but they would have another opportunity. For Jim, however, this was devastating. His one shot at becoming an Olympic champion was snatched away from him. Unlike the other athletes, Jim could not wait another four years.

Jim's weight-lifting career ended when he was just twenty-two. He went totally blind at the age of twenty-nine.

When his world went dark, Jim moved into a small room in the back of his house. A radio, telephone, and tape recorder became his entire existence. He sat in his little room and began to believe that he might never leave it again. The thought of venturing out into the world as a blind person was terrifying.

He didn't know what he was going to do. All his life he had developed a sense of self by being an athlete, someone who set goals for himself and worked as hard as he could to achieve them.

But now he was blind, helpless, and hopeless.

Jim didn't know who he was any longer. The physical prowess with which he identified to make sense of his life was gone—taken from him at no fault of his own. He was angry and lost. Most of all, Jim was afraid.

As is often the case, the more he allowed fear to overcome him, the less he felt his life had any purpose. Day after day in his cramped room, alone, Jim became more incapacitated by fear and felt as though his motivation for life was slipping away fast. He did not want anyone to help him. He could not speak with his supportive family because he feared they would pity him.

He then realized that *he* was in control, that he possessed the power. It was simply a matter of attitude. Fear, he came to figure, was only as strong as *he* determined it to be—no one else. He had no say in the matter of his lack of vision, but he had all the power to determine how he would *react* to being blind.

So he made a decision.

The best decision you can make is to make a decision.

He was not going to let fear get the best of him. He was not going to let blindness determine his self-worth. After several months in self-imposed exile, Jim came to the conclusion that whatever it was he was afraid of couldn't be worse than spending the rest of his life sitting in the dark—waiting for something to come along and change his life. Slowly, through courage and determination, Jim began to emerge from his cocoon.

He knew it would take time and small steps—literally. His first big accomplishment was taking the fifty-two-foot journey to his mailbox. As he reached out his hand and touched the mailbox, his foot slipped off the curb at the edge of the street. He quickly regained balance and chuckled to himself—the type of sound people make when they have an epiphany, or an "aha" moment. With one foot on the street and the other atop the curb, Jim realized for the very first time something so simple yet incredible, something he had taken for granted in all those years of perfect sight: the street in front of his home could take him anywhere in the world he wanted to go.

He knew this was true because every street is interconnected. One street leads to another, to another, to another, and so on. All that was required to move from place to place was the courage to take the first step.

The step of faith.

Over time, Jim strengthened his faith in himself to overcome not only blindness, but the once incapacitating fear that came with it. He soon ventured farther and farther out of his room and closer and closer to purpose.

He wanted to help others affected by lack of vision. He

started the Narrative Television Network in 1988, which unobtrusively adds the voice of a narrator in between the lines of dialogue in a program. This way, blind or low-vision people can hear what they cannot see. The Narrative Television Network has received an Emmy Award, a Media Access Award, and an International Film and Video Award for its pioneering work in making movies, television, and educational programming accessible to the visually impaired.

Jim began to receive requests to speak in public and share his personal story with the world. He has addressed millions of people in a wide variety of forums, sharing the stage with Zig Ziglar, General Colin Powell, Christopher Reeve, and Tony Robbins. Corporations such as Smith Barney, Merrill Lynch, Million Dollar Round Table, MassMutual Life Insurance Company, Liberty Mutual, and the U.S. Chamber of Commerce have engaged him to speak at their corporate events.

One day when he was on a speaking tour with Dr. Robert Schuller and Dr. Denis Waitley, Schuller said, "Jim, I really think you ought to write a book."

Jim responded, "Doc, I can't even read a book, why should I write a book?"

He never thought he could write one book. He went on to write sixteen!

He wrote his bestselling novel, *The Ultimate Gift,* in just five days, dictating it between meetings and conference calls at the television network. Eight million people worldwide have read *The Ultimate Gift*. Follow-up books included *The Ultimate Life* and the recently completed third book in the series, *The Ultimate Journey*.

Twentieth Century Fox turned *The Ultimate Gift* into a feature film starring James Garner. The movie sends trust-fund baby Jason Stevens on an improbable journey of discovery, during which he has to answer the ultimate question: "What is the relationship between wealth and happiness?" When Jason's wealthy grandfather Howard "Red" Stevens dies, in order to receive his multimillion-dollar inheritance, Jason must complete a "crash course on life," twelve tasks that Red calls "gifts," each designed to teach Jason what is truly important in life.

The Ultimate Life has also been made into a movie. Jim's other books include *The Ultimate Financial Plan*, *The Lamp*, *The Sound of Honor*, *Ultimate Productivity*, and *The Way I See The World*.

Jim Stovall went blind. He lost everything, or so it seemed. By the world's standards, life was pretty much over for him by the age of twenty-nine. No one would have blamed him if he had chosen just to "do what little he was capable of" and accepted the fact that he had been dealt a tough hand by fate.

But the truth is, life was just beginning for Jim when he lost his sight. Although he could no longer see it with his eyes, his world expanded in ways that he could not have possibly imagined as a sighted person.

Some of Jim's most meaningful moments during his journey have happened with his family, who have stood by his side and supported him through everything. His parents see the broad picture, but they also share a more intimate understanding of the blessings Jim has received.

When Jim wrote *The Ultimate Gift* screenplay, he created a young female character who has leukemia and dies in the middle of the story. Although he does not talk too much about it, Jim is the third child in his family. Both of his older siblings passed away. His sister died of leukemia, just like the character he created for the movie.

Jim had not told his parents that he had written this character into *The Ultimate Gift*. He was not sure how to tell them that he used his sister to create a fictional person. When his parents attended the movie premiere, Jim had every intention of telling them. Over dinner before the movie he couldn't find the words. After the meal, his throat closed on him. When they got to the theater, the commotion distracted him. He just could not bring himself to tell them about the character.

When the movie started, Jim was nervous. What would his parents say? Would they be angry with him for sharing something so deeply personal and tragic with the world? Would they be upset that he hadn't told them in advance about the character?

As the credits rolled Jim could see that his mother and father were quite emotional. His mother said to him, "We lost your sister almost fifty years ago, and on that day the only peace I had was the faith that somehow there would be a purpose for her death. It took me all these years to figure out what it was. Today we found what it was. It's this movie and this character."

Moments like this, when Jim has been able to share the tremendous love and respect he has for his parents, have meant more to him than all the success he has had with the books and the films.

Jim Stovall is not happy that he went blind, but he knows that many blessings flowed from his illness. He says, "I've had sight and I've had vision. Sight is a precious gift. Sight tells you where you are and what's around you. But vision is infinitely more valuable, because vision tells you where you could be and what is possible. Enjoy your sight, but treasure your vision."

If Jim were given a choice between sight and vision, which would he take? Without question it would be vision.

"It's interesting, that's a lesson I got from my late, great friend, Ray Charles," Jim explains. "I heard him say once that if he had the opportunity to have his sight back but he had to lose his music he would just stay the way he was. At the time I thought, 'What an amazing statement.' Years later I came to understand it. Sight is good, vision is everything. If I had to choose between the two, I'll take vision every time."

Jim Stovall believes that life itself is the ultimate gift. The way we live our lives and the choices we make are the only tribute we have to the life we've been given. When adversity comes, we can choose to see it as a curse or we can choose to see it as a gift. Like Jim, we will often find that the most difficult thing we'll ever have to face is in many ways also our greatest gift.

Expressing his deepest beliefs, Jim says, "It doesn't seem like it when we're in the middle of the chaos, it just seems like this random attack on our life and our happiness, but when we finally get through the valley and we get to the next mountaintop and we look back, we see this kind of divine order and realize there's no other way this would have worked."

Millions of people have been positively impacted by Jim's books. He receives thousands of fan letters from people across the globe. *The Ultimate Gift* is about taking action, not about entitlement or succumbing to the temptation of self-pity. It's about appreciating what you have and working for what you want in life.

For Jim, *stickability* is being totally sold on who you are and what you're doing. It is what keeps you persevering through the most difficult times. It helps you overcome the fear of never knowing what *might have been* if you just persisted instead of quitting. His belief is that you don't have to commit to the end of the road, you have to commit to one more step, one more effort.

There is always more to be seen than our vision can detect.

HOW CAN YOU DEVELOP AN UNYIELDING FAITH IN YOURSELF TO OVERCOME ANY OBSTACLE?

Know the extent and limitations of your own power.

YOU MAY have heard the famous line from the serenity prayer: "Grant me the serenity to accept the things I cannot change; the courage to change the things I can; and the wisdom to know the difference." It would be understandable for Jim to have spent the rest of his days lamenting that which was out of his control, yet nothing productive would have come of it. Like Jim, we must know what we're capable of changing and what we are not.

Know that only you are in control of your attitude.

THE WAYS in which we respond to our environment are entirely up to us! Jim was dealt a blinding blow, literally, at no fault of his own. He could not simply choose to see, but he chose to have a positive attitude about it. This empowered him with the *vision* that even blindness cannot diminish his capabilities. You can only persist in the face of challenges with an opportunistic, positive attitude. If you think the obstacle is too large to overcome, it is!

Take small steps.

YOU HAVE big goals, we all do. Keep them! We owe it to ourselves to dream big. Just know, however, that the bigger the goal the more steps we must take to achieve it—and the most difficult is the very first one. The smaller the steps you take toward your goal, the better positioned you will be to sidestep the obstacles along the way. Focus on the next step, then the one after, then the one after that. You may find, like Jim, that your steps will lead you to a place better than you ever envisioned.

CHAPTER 11

Innovation Through Necessity

—◦⁄◦⁄◦—

"STEVE, MEET STEVE."

And the rest is history.

Not so fast . . . who are these Steves and how did they make history?

One Steve is a household name—the late Steve Jobs. This is the story of the second one.

In 1970, rising college sophomore Steve Wozniak—or Woz—spent his summer vacation building a mainframe computer for Hewlett-Packard. This is where he met Steve Jobs. Just one year after enrolling in school, Wozniak withdrew from UC Berkeley and developed the computer that would make both Steves famous.

"The way I grew up," Wozniak said in an interview, "I was

designing a bunch of stuff very young and because I couldn't ever get the money to build it, I had to design it over and over and over. I made up a game. The game was: *Can I do it with fewer pieces than before?*"

The reason for this was he was too poor to afford a lot of game pieces—also known as computer chips and drives—so he *had* to do more with less. It was a matter of necessity that became the driving motivator.

Do what you know—with what you have.

Steve elaborated on his "Keep It Simple, Stupid" (KISS) philosophy:

"I looked at the architecture of a computer and worked out the very fewest pieces that would work. I came up with tricks that weren't in any book; they were so unusual, they were using parts in ways they weren't supposed to be used but it was all to make it simpler and smaller. Because I got very good at this, I was actually designing computers that were using half as many chips as the manufacturers. I knew I was very good at it. I made it a value to me: make things simpler and smaller!"

By himself, Steve designed the hardware, circuit boards, and operating system for the Apple I. With the Apple I design, Steve Wozniak and Steve Jobs were largely working to impress other members of the Palo Alto–based Homebrew Computer Club, which was a group of electronics hobbyists interested in computing. The club was one of several key centers that established the home hobbyist era, essentially creating the micro-computer industry over several years. Unlike other Homebrew designs, the Apple had a simple video capability that drew a crowd when the machine was unveiled.

According to Wozniak's autobiography, *iWoz*, he and Steve Jobs sold some of their possessions, including Wozniak's HP scientific calculator and Jobs's Volkswagen van, for $1,300 and assembled the first Apple circuit boards in Jobs's bedroom and later in his garage. Wozniak's apartment in San Jose was filled with monitors, electronic devices, and some computer games he had developed.

On April 1, 1976, Jobs and Wozniak formed Apple Computer. Apple's first personal computer, the Apple I, was purely a hobbyist machine. Wozniak single-handedly designed the Apple II, which was the first personal computer that had the ability to display color graphics. The Apple II became one of the first highly successful mass-produced personal computers.

As of April 2012, Apple's market value was $586.8 billion, making it the most valuable corporation on the planet, far above the previous leader, Exxon Mobil Corporation, which was valued at $404.5 billion.

Fun facts . . .

Apple's market value is now worth more than: the total annual retail sales of electricity in the United States, the entire National Football League—times ten—the construction of the United States interstate-highway system, the entire value of the United States stock market circa 1977, and more than the gross domestic product of Poland, Belgium, Saudi Arabia, Sweden, and Taiwan.

Many analysts predict that, in the coming decade, Apple Computer will be the first company ever to exceed $1 trillion in sales.

All of this success, this tremendous wealth and staggering innovation, came as the direct result of two guys with a vision and very little else. In fact, Apple's success, according to Wozniak, was possible only because they had one very important thing in addition to a great vision: *necessity*.

"We worked with what we had," Wozniak explains. "We had almost no money, Steve Jobs and me, so we had to figure out ways to build things that cost almost nothing. It forced us to think and come up with new approaches. If we'd had all the money in the world, we might have just been satisfied buying things the way they were, just becoming another so-so company. By the time we actually made it at Apple, I looked back at all of the little projects I had worked on, one after another, and other totally wacko ideas the world had never seen in computers—every one of them came about largely because I had no money. I had to figure out ways to do things with just a few one-dollar chips. I could not just do things in the standard way that you learn in a book."

Today we are accustomed to inserting a flash drive into a USB port and downloading data in megabyte chunks. But someone had to invent the first widely used mobile data-storage device.

That someone was Steve Wozniak.

"When I created the first floppy disk I had to simplify things out of necessity. Necessity can be the mother of all invention. I didn't know how to make a floppy disk. I had never worked with the software of a disk operating system, but I had a strong motivating factor. If I got it built in two weeks and it worked and I could store programs on a floppy disk and read them back in and run them, I got to go to Las Vegas.

"The first thing I did on day one was study this little Shugart drive that Steve Jobs thought was hot. He wanted to move this smaller drive into computers. I studied all their circuitry and saw what it did. You're supposed to send them a language, a language of wires with signals of voltages, and that language got translated by all these chips and caused two things to happen: a head would move up or down, in or out on the tracks, and you'd write data or you'd read data. Simple, simple! So I said, 'Wait a minute, why don't I just run one wire over to write the data and one wire over to get the data that's received?' That way I could send data directly from my little card and skip twenty of the chips Shugart had built into their own disk. Steve Jobs liked that because it gave us a reason to offer a better price. I always think minimally, that's my way in life."

For Steve Wozniak, *stickability* has everything to do with pursuing his passion. Like many brilliant inventors and innovators, fame and financial success are the by-products, not the prime motivating factors behind his efforts.

"All I wanted credit for was being a great engineer and for having designed the products, and I get that credit no matter what. I'm not a person who wants to put himself out in front of the world. I don't want fame. I don't understand people who come up to me and want autographs. In the early days of Apple I said, 'I just did a good engineering job, I'm a great engineer.' I'm not a Hollywood celebrity. What is going on with this? All this celebrity attention that I get, I like it because people are nice, but I don't understand it exactly. Everybody that's working on the iPod or the iPhone, they are doing incredible stuff, but you have never heard of their names. I think that's largely because once you have an established company, the company wants to take credit for the product in a certain way. There's a way it has to present it and market it and there isn't much room to develop new technical heroes. But there are a few, more than a few."

What does the future hold for technology?

Steve has a vision, and that's why he joined the information-technology company Fusion-io. They are doing now what Steve did when he was young. They look for ways to innovate, not re-create.

"At Fusion-io we looked at the problem of how do you replace a hard disk with all its spinning materials and atoms with light little chips that just run tiny little electrons around to store your data, store your music, store everything? This technology is the future. It's actually almost the present. It's already sort of happened with the big hard disks that serve all the data that we get on the Internet. Whenever we're on the Internet we're doing stuff coming off these big data centers. They've almost all been converted over to our style of technology.

"But this company didn't just build a simpler device by taking a hard disk and making it electronic, they plugged the electronics into the computer and wrote some software to make it seem like the disk of old. Now, with the disk of old, you'd have a card in a computer with a fiber cable off to a big chasse. These are expensive things—big racks of computers with hard disks plugged in and RAID arrays to share the data. All of that is gone. One card would replace about a hundred-thousand-dollar rack of computers and disk drives. I thought, 'This is the sort of simplicity I live for,' and where I learned that, yeah, it was at Apple. I learned the value of simplicity early on.

"Some of the most complex things in life can be reduced to being very simple," Steve explains. "The way we think at a very high level, everything in the world seems very simple to us. That's a telephone, that's a chair. The amount of processing that's involved in a brain is actually incredible. Now we have to build these kinds of things into our computer equipment. That is a difficult challenge involving millions of lines of code."

What does Steve want his legacy to be? That he helped to create the biggest corporation on the planet? That the public treated him like a rock star?

No. Steve prefers to think of legacy in terms of the tangible effects his work and innovation have on the everyday lives of people.

"I wish my legacy was that I had managed to get a home and a car and a family and some kids and send them to school—you know, the normal things in life. But the truth is I am a great engineer. I did my best to figure out things that other people couldn't figure out. I came up with the formula to make personal computers that people could own. I care so much about people in their homes. I want them to own the great stuff. It shouldn't be only the military and the big corporations who get good computers."

Steve understands that people love to hear his story because, let's face it, he changed the world! The world, in fact, is full of dreamers and hardworking innovators, but what separates the good from the great?

Stickability.

Great innovators put people first. Like Steve, they never quit on their dreams, and in the face of challenges they focus on the lasting effects their accomplishments will have on others— and in Steve's case, on humanity!

Most of us cannot do what Steve did—neither Wozniak nor Jobs, to be sure. It's important to remember, however, that they likely cannot do what you can do! Whatever your vision is, get up each and every day and give it the best you have to make it a reality. Learn from your mistakes and always seek to reach the next level.

And do not be afraid of *necessity*. We all want to be in a state of surplus—financially or otherwise. Too often we fear being *in need* and fail to see the opportunities available to us.

For us non-techies, *this* is what we can learn from Steve Wozniak. Steve knows that people will probably remember him most for Apple Computer. Better than anyone   with the possible exception of his late friend Steve Jobs—Steve Wozniak knows and appreciates just how special Apple Computer was and still is, especially in the minds of the millions of people who use Apple's products every day.

"I know the stories people like to hear. How did we turn our ideas into reality? Those early days mattered a lot. I think a lot of people want to be entrepreneurs. They want to be able to go out with their own ideas, start something and create something that's incredibly valuable. I can't say that we foresaw the mega-success Apple became but, boy, we sure thought that we were onto something big."

"Woz" is truly a living legend. He has received numerous accolades and honorary degrees. He has appeared as a guest on popular television shows like *The Big Bang Theory* and *Dancing with the Stars*. One term used to describe him is "cultural icon."

But, if you ask him, Steve will tell you that he is simply a great engineer with a vision and the *stickability* to turn his dreams into reality.

WHAT ARE THE KEYS TO INNOVATION?

Have confidence in your abilities.

MORE SPECIFIC than having faith in yourself, it is vital to know unequivocally what you can bring to the table—and what you cannot. Know your craft, whatever it may be, and hone it to the highest level possible.

Be an expert at what you love to do, and make no apologies for your greatness. Having confidence is not the same as being arrogant. Know the difference.

Keep It Simple, Stupid.

GREAT INNOVATORS make our world more efficient. They are able to see a problem and, like Steve Wozniak did with the personal computer, simplify it to provide solutions. Ask yourself, "What process or product in my world is too complex, inefficient, or poorly conceived? How can I make it better?" This takes discipline and will—to remain focused on the steps that are necessary, and only those steps, and not try to do it all at once. *Moderation is the ultimate exercise of willpower.*

Create the need.

STEVE WOZNIAK was not satisfied with the *way things had always been* when it came to computers. In order to truly innovate, you must identify a need that is not currently met and fulfill it creatively. Wherever there is a need, there is an opportunity for improvement. Innovators are able to think beyond traditional models and execute their visions!

CHAPTER 12

Second Act

IN HIS CLASSIC BOOK *Think and Grow Rich*, NAPOLEON
Hill offered thirteen dynamite principles based on his already
well-regarded Laws of Success that had intrigued many of the
most powerful and wealthy men of his time—including presi-
dents, political leaders, educators, and business magnates.
When the book was published in 1937, Hill himself experienced
a new level of success and fame that placed him in the pantheon
of heroes for those of us who believe in following in the foot-
steps of the truly great thinkers and achievers of the past.

At his core, Hill never forgot that he came from poverty—
the dirt-poor kind of destitution few of us can understand
today. Like Steve Wozniak in the previous chapter, he over-
came grinding poverty and was an entirely self-made, up-

by-the-bootstraps kind of person. And just as he knew what the world looked like from the pinnacle of success, he also experienced failures and setbacks all along the way. He came back from each, rose higher every time, and applied the lessons learned to motivate him and make him stronger.

Hill believed in second acts. (And even third and fourth acts . . .)

Of course, we all fail from time to time. The higher we aim, the lower we can fall if we don't succeed. But failure is the crucial time of testing for leaders and truly successful men and women.

One thing is certain: you are preventing yourself from succeeding if you don't even try. Think of the men who hesitated when offered a *guaranteed* opportunity and who lost out on that opportunity because they couldn't even make a decision to *try*. Think of that thirty-second moment when Napoleon Hill sat with Andrew Carnegie and could have said "maybe" to the chance that changed his life—and uplifted the lives of so many others. . . .

Whatever the outside conditions, the source of success lies within each of us. That was one of Hill's greatest insights and one reason his writings and his philosophy remain so alive today. And he was right! He saw:

"If the thing you wish to do is right, and *you believe in it*, go ahead and do it! Put your dream across, and never mind what 'they' say if you meet with temporary defeat, for 'they,' perhaps, do not know that EVERY FAILURE BRINGS WITH IT THE SEED OF AN EQUIVALENT SUCCESS."

Hill went on to write, prophetically:

"The majority of people are ready to throw their aims and purposes overboard, and give up at the first sign of opposition or misfortune. A few carry on despite all opposition, until they attain their goal. These few are the Fords, Carnegies, Rockefellers, and Edisons."

Those were the titans of the early twentieth century. Their stories are well-known to us. Their examples of the principle of *stickability* are already in the history books. But we're looking at some of the shining stars of today and sharing their stories, even as they are still making history, still competing in the arena.

Life is a contact sport. Get in there and play.

Enter Mike Muhney (pronounced myoo-NIH, as in "municipal"), coinventor of ACT! (originally standing for Activity Control Technology) and strategic reinventor of himself. When we had the chance to talk to him about his story—maybe we should say stories, plural—one thing came through loud and clear: his passion about what he does. He is a self-described "sales guy" who went out on a limb one day with a friend and had a brainstorm that resulted in a multimillion-dollar idea that became an industry.

He and a partner had started up a software company with a $100,000 investment from an angel. "We worked through $85,000 of that and said this dog ain't going to hunt. We were desperate, and I talked to a mentor and he said hey, you guys go out to breakfast and brainstorm." That's exactly what they did. They met for breakfast and had an intense conversation. They knew sales and wondered how to convert winning sales principles to software. They wrote down the idea on a piece of paper—which Mike still has.

What did he do? He created a new business category: "contact management." He also invented the name ACT!, which marketing gurus said had defined the field and forced competitors who enter the game to refer to or use your product and its name because they would be in the contact-management category.

He likes to say, "Life is a contact sport." And he means it.

"Let's be street smart here," Mike says. "What are your strengths? I work out to get physically stronger. The whole purpose is to be stronger. Why wouldn't I do the same in my job or business pursuits?"

He said that after he sold ACT!: "It was the best of times; it was the worst of times. We actually got fired by Symantec four months after they acquired us. They told us to shut up and do our jobs. I lost a lot, including my marriage relationship. I was alone. I was despondent. I lost balance. The success of ACT! put so much attention on me that I lost balance in my real relationships."

Knowing what he knows now, would he do it over again?

"Of course I would. To say otherwise would be foolish. I lost balance. The attention and success put so much focus on me, I lost balance in my personal life. I would put greater intensity and focus on the balance in my life."

Three years later, he felt extremely irrelevant. He retired at forty-two, but asked himself, "What is my life's destiny supposed to be?" As time passed, he became more irrelevant to the people around him. He felt that way, and says, "I know if I felt that way, I must have appeared that way to other people too. There was something missing. There wasn't a sense of confidence that I once had when I was involved with ACT!"

He needed a new mission, a new goal. He needed to reinvent Mike Muhney.

"Actually, I started a company with Michael Jordan and Charles Barkley in June 1996. The company failed because Michael went back into basketball and wasn't able to devote his time to the new venture. So I was foundering again! What was I going to do with my time when all my other friends were working . . . ? So I just had this spiral down when nothing I had to do was meaningful to me. I wasn't enjoying anything."

His greatest success, ACT!, was over. Everything he did afterward seemed anticlimactic. So what would he do next? Retirement wasn't for him at such a young age. The thrill of the hunt, the yearning for competition and accomplishment called him. It still does.

For Mike, the answer lay in something he had heard from a wise friend:

Success should be a springboard—not a hammock!

What would he do differently?

"I have a rebellious gene, I have an antiauthoritarian chromosome. I don't follow conventional wisdom. I want to be in charge. I want to make a difference. And I want to be what I'm supposed to be. I'm not there yet. It's a force in me, a yearning."

When challenged about how much is really new in what he is doing now, Mike Muhney smiles. When pushed, he likes to push back. That's what *stickability* means to him.

He says, "Despite coinventing ACT!, which is a Windows product, I no longer use it because I converted to Apple in

2004. I bought the first iPhone and after two years of using it I longed for the same robust relationship-management productivity on a device that was now with me 24/7. So, I saw another opportunity to create what I once did with ACT! But this time it would be designed for mobile devices and bring the same value proposition to not only myself but to other mobile-device users who would want that power on their devices as well. So, I invented VIPorbit, and along with it created an even bigger category called 'mobile relationship management' and even went beyond ACT! with what it helped me to do better in all of my relationship-centric activities. I'm like a kid in a candy store because I'm using my expertise, which is about relationship management, and I'm back on the right path. But I'm not where I should be.

"I want to change the world. I want to conquer the world and I look at ACT! as nothing more than a successful experiment to now move on to higher planes with VIPorbit. I set my goals impossibly high and stretch myself to get to that impossibly high level as much as I possibly can."

He easily shares his elevator pitch: "What we're developing is the best way to manage your contacts, calendars, and communications. It is your on-demand, instant-recall, photographic-memory executive assistant."

You can feel the passion and enthusiasm radiating from him

when he talks about his goals and his strategies to achieve them. That's one thing that cuts through the obstacles skeptics and even well-meaning friends and family will throw in the way of the entrepreneur's big idea.

So what do you do when there are close friends and relatives telling you that you can't do it?

"You have to look for realism in your idea . . . that people could use this—that *we* could use this. You have to listen, but you have to know in your heart that you're onto something. Then we realized [the skeptics and naysayers] were irrelevant in their close-mindedness. If they're not going to help you, get 'em out of the way."

Instinct is a tool that can help overcome opposition. Trust your gut. That's what Mike Muhney has in spades—as do other world-class achievers.

Mike's nuggets of wisdom are not revolutionary, but they are heartfelt and born of experience, and he expresses himself with that trademark passion when he talks about what he's learned from the first half of his life that will take him through the second half—and the second act. He's always looking forward.

First: "Personally, I have learned that I have to believe in myself. I can't tell you how many times I've had to call on a reservoir in my own heart, in the motion of my mind and my soul, just to keep going. I've always forced myself to believe in myself.

"It's kind of a cliché, but second, don't give up. I can't ever give up on myself. Keep after it until you've exhausted it and know it was never meant to be."

For him, that is the essence of *stickability,* and he finds incredible inspiration in the poet John Greenleaf Whittier, who wrote:

Of all the sad words of tongue or pen,
The saddest are these: "It might have been."

"I don't want to come to the end of my life and say that I wish I had done that thing. Why was I afraid of it? Forget your fears and go after what you believe in and want to try. Even if you fail, that means you've tried."

And for Mike Muhney, failure—after trying your hardest—is the step forward that leads to the second act, or even the third or fourth act . . . whatever act you're willing to write for yourself on the path to ultimate success.

—◦◦◦—

All it requires is some good old-fashioned *stickability*! What does this mean?

You are your own best customer.

ONE KEY takeaway from Mike Muhney's experience is that he invented a product that *he* needed and wanted. Say to yourself, "What would I spend my own money on to make my life happier or my business efforts more profitable? What do I need?" Then make your answer happen!

SOMEBODY thought of the idea of the little sliding tray in a kitty litter box. Somebody thought of that to make their life easier and made it happen. Your needs can be the catalyst for your idea and invention.

You are your own toughest competitor.

SETTING GOALS and stretching to achieve them pits you against yourself at least as much as (if not more than) external competition. What you achieved yesterday is the measure by which you are judged today. For the successful entrepreneur and leader, that means the bar is continually being raised. Mike cites a favorite saying, to this effect: "The only competition worthy of a wise man is with himself."

CHALLENGE YOURSELF. Compete with yourself. Beat yourself to the finish line.

Your gut and your ideas will get you where you want to be.

SO DON'T abandon them. They've been good to you. They have inspired and energized you. That's what gives you passion and direction. Whether it's a God-given spark or a pain in your neck (literal or figurative), it is a sign that your creative juices are flowing. Go with your strength! Listen to legitimate criticism and learn. But don't let those well-meaning others derail your train. Never lose focus, and never lose hope.

Do whatever is out there to do—for you.

HARRY S. TRUMAN said, "Men make history, and not the other way around." Yes, you can change the world. Every change started with an idea. Explore yours.

Afterword

THREE FEET FROM GOLD

As Dr. Napoleon Hill described it,

One of the most common causes of failure is the habit of quitting when one is overtaken by temporary defeat.

Every person is guilty of this mistake at one time or another.

He illustrated the point with the story of R. U. Darby and his uncle, who toiled and drilled for weeks upon weeks to discover a vein of gold in Colorado only to have it run out after the first quick return.

The Darbys then quit and sold their mining equipment to a junk man for a few hundred dollars.

Some "junk men" are dumb, but not this one. He called in a mining engineer to look at the mine and do a little calculating. . . . His calculations showed that the vein would be found JUST THREE FEET FROM WHERE THE DARBYS HAD STOPPED DRILLING!

That junk man became a millionaire, and Darby (who later became a millionaire in the insurance industry by never quitting again) learned the lesson of a lifetime, which resonates for us today.

How many times have we, or someone we know, quit one class short of a degree, given up on sales too early, or lost faith in something we truly desired?

Like Darby, the entrepreneurs and inventors in this book profited from the lesson by saying to themselves:

I will never again stop three feet from gold because others say "no" or "that won't work" or "you're crazy to keep trying."

For the experts featured in this book, the idea of quitting three feet from gold would probably not even occur, but for most of us regular, everyday mortals that may not be the case.

We have to learn to develop the habits and practices that

will move us beyond the fears and limitations that hold most of us back and keep us from digging and drilling for that mother lode that lies before us.

From meeting with many of the greatest intellectual minds of our generation, one overwhelming success principle rings true. Perseverance will, ultimately, carry us through to the achievement of *our* dream.

Les Brown, who is known as The Motivator, always says there is greatness within us. A special gift, talent, or purpose that the world is waiting to hear.

Let this book become the catalyst to turn that passion into reality.

Although we may have never met—this is guaranteed. For the past few years, you have been taking care of your family, friends, peers, etc., and have been placing the needs of others before your own.

Now it's *your* turn. It's your turn to experience, learn, and the take the first steps toward creating a life of sustained abundance.

It's time to put away the excuses for what hasn't happened in the past and begin searching the possibilities for what the future holds.

It's time to adopt the *courage to succeed* explained by four-time Olympian Rubén González:

The courage to get started, and once you get started, the courage to not quit.

Yes, there will be challenges, and yes, there will be pain. The key is to keep focused on what matters most and stay the course through oncoming storms.

Once you're close to the finish line, keep going, keep shining, and keep running.

You have greatness within you.

Find your *stickability*, hang in there, and never give up.

After all, you could be Three Feet from Gold.

Thank you for reading this, best wishes, and whatever you do . . .

Keep smiling ☺

Please let me know how I may be of service.

Greg S. Reid

Acknowledgments

THIS BOOK IS DEDICATED TO THE DREAMERS, BELIEV-
ers, and achievers who discovered that true success comes
from . . .

Turning our obstacles into opportunities.

Thank you to our writing staff who made this project the
best form of itself:

Shamayah Sarrucco—Greg Tobin—Summer Felix—Josh
Rosenthal.

We thank the fans of Napoleon Hill's work and teachings
who preserve his legacy by supporting only authorized Napoleon Hill Foundation publications and programs.

Special appreciation goes out to the author's personal Mastermind group who supported this project during the journey and joined in the quest:

Clarissa Burt—Deborah Ives—Flor Mazeda—Forrest May—Maria Gamb

Glen and Natalie Ledwell—Steve Sougstad—Tara Henson—Lori Taylor

Luba Rusyn—Misha Elias—Richard Barrier—Travis Houston

Terri Simpson—Savannah Ross—Allyn Reid—Don Green—David Corbin

About the Author

GREG S. REID is a filmmaker, motivational speaker, and best-selling author. He is also an entrepreneur, and the CEO of several successful corporations, who has dedicated his life to helping others achieve the ultimate fulfillment of finding and living a life of purpose. Visit him online at www.BookGreg.com.

NAPOLEON HILL was born in 1883 in Wise County, Virginia. He began his writing career at age thirteen as a "mountain reporter" for small-town newspapers and went on to become America's most beloved motivational author. His work stands as a monument to individual achievement and is the cornerstone of modern motivation. His most famous work, *Think and*

Grow Rich, is one of the best-selling books of all time. Hill established The Napoleon Hill Foundation as a nonprofit educational institution whose mission is to perpetuate his philosophy of leadership, self-motivation, and individual achievement. Visit The Napoleon Hill Foundation online at www.naphill.org.

—◦◦◦—

To learn more about the featured experts, and to stay in touch with the author, visit www.Stick-Ability.com.

Claim your bonus gift of Napoleon Hill's audio *Three Causes of Failure* at www.StickabilityBook.com

If you enjoyed this book, visit

www.tarcherbooks.com

and sign up for Tarcher's e-newsletter to receive special offers, giveaway promotions, and information on hot upcoming releases.

TARCHER
PENGUIN

Great Lives Begin with Great Ideas

Connect with the Tarcher Community

• • •

Stay in touch with favorite authors!
Enter weekly contests!
Read exclusive excerpts!
Voice your opinions!

Follow us

 Tarcher Books

 @TarcherBooks

If you would like to place a bulk order
of this book, call 1-800-847-5515.